Intermediate Faster Reading
―New Edition―

速読の実践演習
―最新版―

Casey Malarcher

原　田　慎　一

photographs by	写真・資料提供
Jiji Press Photo	時事通信フォト

音声ファイルのダウンロード/ストリーミング

CDマーク表示がある箇所は、音声を弊社HPより無料でダウンロード/ストリーミングすることができます。トップページのバナーをクリックし、書籍検索してください。書籍詳細ページに音声ダウンロードアイコンがございますのでそちらから自習用音声としてご活用ください。

https://www.seibido.co.jp

ALL RIGHTS RESERVED The Japanese edition Copyright © 2015 by Seibido Publishing Co., Ltd.

The original text © 2012 was published by Cengage Learning Asia Pte Ltd.

No part of this work covered by the copyright hereon may be reproduced or used in any form or by any means—graphic, electronic or mechanical, including photocopying, recording, taping, web distribution or information storage and retrieval systems—without the written permission of the publisher.

本書のねらい

　本書は、好評を頂いた『速読の実践演習 Intermediate Faster Reading』（Casey Malarcher、森田　彰、原田　慎一）の最新版です。慈善活動・ICT・大都市など最近の話題を扱ったpassageを第2版のものから一部入れ替え、より興味深い内容にいたしました。

　基本語彙で書かれた比較的やさしい英文を読み、内容理解やリスニングの問題を解きながらリーディング力や語彙力を養成できるよう編集された総合教材です。問題の難易度を抑えていますので、英語を苦手とする方に適しています。passageのジャンルは多岐に渡っており、楽しみながら読み進めることができる内容になっています。

　本書は、1課4ページの計20課の構成になっています。1ページ目では、日本語の導入による内容スキーマ（背景知識）の構築と、重要語の意味の確認を行います。この2つのアクティビティにより、本文の内容理解が容易になります。2ページ目で300語程度のpassageを読みます。最新版から重要語や注の語句はゴシック体に変更し、本文のどこで使われているのかが一目瞭然となっています。3ページ目には、内容理解の問題と要約のリスニング問題があります。内容理解問題は、4択のやさしい問題ですが、本文をきちんと理解していないと間違えてしまう適度な難易度になっています。リスニングはやや難易度が上がりますが、本文と照らし合わせながら聴くとよいと思います。最後の4ページ目で、重要語句の再確認を行い、定着を図ります。

　速読力を鍛えるために、各passageの語数を読み終えた時間で割り、1分間当たりに読むことができる語数（WPM）を算出するのも効果的です。1課から20課までのWPMを記録し、速読力の伸長度を可視化するとやる気が出ると思います。

　本書は速読テキストですが、文の構造を把握しながら読む精読にも適しています。英文は平易に書かれていますが、関係詞・不定詞・動名詞・分詞など様々な文法項目を含んでいます。速読しようとするとpassageの理解がおろそかになるという人は、英文を正確に読むことを優先しましょう。精読の力がつけば、読む速度も自然と速くなります。

　本書の20課を読み終えれば、まとまった英語の文章を読みこなす自信がつくはずです。本書の使い方をよく読んで、楽しみながら学習してください。

　最後に、本書の編集・出版に際して、有益なご助言と多大なご尽力を賜った成美堂の菅野英一氏に心より感謝申し上げます。

2015年7月

編著者

本書の使い方

BEFORE YOU READ
　最初に、本文の内容理解を助ける日本語の簡単な導入があります。導入は本文を読むときのヒントになっています。写真を見ながら、どんな内容が書いてあるのか予測してみてください。

TARGET VOCABULARY
　本文を読む前に、本文で使用されている重要語の意味を確認します。まず、日本語で意味を書いてみて、自信のない語句や知らない語句は辞書で調べてみましょう。次に、それらの定義や同義語がやさしい英語で書かれていますから、それを結びつけて、語句のイメージも定着させてみましょう。

READING PASSAGE
　本文は比較的やさしい単語を使って書かれた300語程度の英文です。自分のレベルに合わせて、読み方を変えるといいでしょう。本文をやさしいと思う人は、時間を計りながら全体の内容を短時間で読み取る速読をしてみましょう。その際にはわからない単語があっても辞書を引かずに、全体の流れから意味を類推しながら読み進めましょう。本文の最後に単語数があります。読み終えたら、単語数を読むのにかかった時間で割ります。例えば、300語の文を6分で読み終えた場合、300語÷6分＝分速50語です。毎回、分速を記録しておけば、速読力の伸びがわかります。本文を難しいと思う人は、冒頭の語彙問題や注の説明に加え、必要に応じて辞書を使うといいでしょう。1文1文時間をかけ、最終的に話の内容が理解できたときの喜びは非常に大きいと思います。本書を終えた後は、以前よりもリーディング力や語彙力が身につき、英語を読むことが楽しくなっているはずです。

READING COMPREHENSION
　リーディング後に本文をきちんと理解していたかどうかを5問の選択問題で確認します。全体的な内容を問う問題もあれば、詳細な内容を問う問題もあります。本文に書かれていないものを選択させるNOT問題は要注意です。自信がない場合は、本文に戻って、解答の根拠となる箇所を探しましょう。

LISTENING COMPREHENSION
　本文の内容の要約をリスニングし、空所に語句を入れ、要約を完成させます。少し難易度が高いアクティビティです。音声を聴いてもわからない場合や、語句が聴き取れてもスペルがわからない場合は、本文を読み返して確認してみましょう。完成した要約を何度も音読し暗記すれば、英語で短い話をするスピーキング力が身につきます。

VOCABULARY REINFORCEMENT
　本文で出てきた重要語句の使い方を選択問題で確認します。問題の形式は、文脈に当てはまる語句を空所に入れるものと、イタリック体の語句の同義語を選ぶものがあります。例文と一緒に覚え、スピーキングやライティングに使えるようにするといい

でしょう。

IDIOMS

本文で使われたイディオムのうち、特に使用頻度が高く、重要と思われる3つのイディオムをピックアップしています。例文を和訳し、その意味を文の中で確認してください。

CONTENTS

Unit 1　**Coffee Culture** 1
　　　　（スターバックス）

Unit 2　**Helping Others** 5
　　　　（慈善活動）

Unit 3　**Movie Directors** 9
　　　　（映画監督）

Unit 4　**Around the World** 13
　　　　（世界一周）

Unit 5　**Yuna Kim** 17
　　　　（キム・ヨナ）

Unit 6　**The Puffer Fish** 21
　　　　（フグの毒に要注意）

Unit 7　**Technology in the Classroom** 25
　　　　（教室でコンピューターを使おう）

Unit 8　**Interesting Buildings** 29
　　　　（変わった建物）

Unit 9　**Bollywood** 33
　　　　（新映画の都　ボリウッド）

Unit 10　**The Nobel Prize** 37
　　　　（ノーベル賞）

Unit 11　**A Funny Cure** 41
　　　　（珍しい治療法）

Unit 12　**Palm Reading** 45
　　　　（手相を見ましょう）

Unit 13　**Amazing Memory** 49
　　　　（驚異の記憶力）

Unit 14　**Incredible Dogs** 53
　　　　（ワンダフルわんちゃん）

Unit 15　**Megacities** 57
　　　　（大都市）

Unit 16　**Space Explorers** 61
　　　　（宇宙飛行士）

Unit 17　**Happy New Year!** 65
　　　　（ハッピーニューイヤー）

Unit 18　**Rain** 69
　　　　（レイン）

Unit 19　**Urban Legends** 73
　　　　（都市伝説はホント？　ウソ？）

Unit 20　**Extreme Sports** 77
　　　　（極限のスポーツ）

Word Per Minute 記録シート 81

Coffee Culture

スターバックス

皆さんは普段コーヒーをどのくらい飲みますか。今回はスターバックスの話です。日本では「スタバ」の愛称で親しまれ、いたるところでその店舗を見かけますが、スターバックスの発祥の地はどこなのでしょうか。また、その歴史はどのようなものなのでしょうか。なんだかコーヒーを飲みながら話を読んでみたくなりましたね。

TARGET VOCABULARY

Look up each word in a dictionary and match it with the closest meaning.

1. _____ atmosphere   ( ) a. give someone a job
2. _____ casual   ( ) b. manage (e.g., a company)
3. _____ create   ( ) c. make something for the first time
4. _____ hire   ( ) d. the feeling created by furniture, lights, music, etc
5. _____ run (something)   ( ) e. relaxed; not formal

READING PASSAGE

1   Although people everywhere seem to enjoy drinking coffee, they do not all have the same coffee culture. In Europe, for example, coffee shops are common places for people to meet friends and to talk while they drink coffee. On the other hand, locations like this were not as common in North America in the past. Instead, people in North
5   America tended to drink coffee in their homes with their friends. The coffee culture in the USA changed when Starbucks coffee shops spread across the country.

   The first Starbucks coffee shop opened in 1971 in downtown Seattle, Washington, in the USA. It was a small coffee shop that roasted its own coffee beans. The coffee shop's business did well, and by 1981 there were three more Starbucks stores in
10   Seattle.

   Things really began to change for the company in 1981. That year, Howard Schultz met the three men who **ran** Starbucks. Schultz worked in New York for a company that made kitchen equipment. He noticed that Starbucks ordered **a large number** of special coffee makers and he was curious. Schultz went to Seattle to see what
15   Starbucks did. In 1982, the original Starbucks owners **hired** Schultz as the company's head of **marketing**.

   In 1983, Schultz traveled to Italy. The unique **atmosphere** of the espresso bars there caught his eye. Back in the USA, Schultz **created** an atmosphere for Starbucks coffee shops that was comfortable and **casual**, and customers everywhere seemed to
20   like it. Starbucks began opening more locations across the USA. Then the company opened coffee shops in other countries as well. Today, there are more than 16,000 Starbucks coffee shops worldwide.

   However, that does not mean Starbucks has not had problems. As a matter of fact, many Starbucks locations have closed over the past few years. In some cases, this is
25   because there were too many coffee shops competing for business in one small area. In other cases, locations in some countries closed because the coffee culture there did not match with the "**feel the same everywhere**" atmosphere offered by Starbucks.

                                                                            341 words

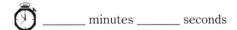

a large number of「多数の」　**marketing**「マーケティング」(商品・サービスなどの売り上げを増加させるために実施される市場調査.)　**espresso**「エスプレッソ」(細かく挽いたコーヒー豆を圧搾蒸気を用いて短時間で抽出したもの.)　**feel the same everywhere**「どこにいても同じように感じる」

READING COMPREHENSION

Circle the letter of the best answer.

1. What is the main topic of the passage?
   a. how a company has grown
   b. what can be added to coffee
   c. the kind of coffee that customers like
   d. how to make coffee

2. Which is NOT true about Starbucks' first ten years of business?
   a. It opened only three stores.
   b. It was not run by Howard Schultz.
   c. Its head of marketing lived in New York.
   d. It roasted its own beans.

3. Who is Howard Schultz?
   a. a coffee seller from New York
   b. an Italian coffee maker
   c. the man who changed the company
   d. one of the original owners of Starbucks

4. Which of the following is true according to the passage?
   a. Starbucks closed most of its US shops.
   b. There are 16,000 Starbucks in the US.
   c. Schultz no longer works for the company.
   d. It is in thousands of locations worldwide.

5. What led to the closing of some Starbucks locations?
   a. all of the coffee tastes the same
   b. cultures that do not drink coffee
   c. selling drinks that are too expensive
   d. too many coffee shops in one place

LISTENING COMPREHENSION 03

Listen to the CD and fill in the blanks.

Starbucks began as a small coffee company in (1) _____ Seattle in the United States. A man in New York noticed the small company bought a lot of special equipment to make coffee. He went to Seattle to learn about the company and was later (2)_____ by Starbucks. This man changed the (3)_____ of the stores and helped to make Starbucks a huge company. (4)_____, Starbucks today has stores in thousands of (5)_____ in countries worldwide.

3

VOCABULARY REINFORCEMENT

Circle the letter of the words that best match the words in *italics*.

1. The bright lights *caught his eye*.
   - a. made him look
   - b. scared him
   - c. saw him
   - d. upset him

2. Put the meat in the oven and *roast* it for two hours.
   - a. eat
   - b. cook
   - c. serve
   - d. hire

3. The director *created* a beautiful movie with very little money.
   - a. bought
   - b. changed
   - c. made
   - d. opened

4. The meeting yesterday was very *casual*.
   - a. mixed
   - b. new
   - c. professional
   - d. relaxed

5. My uncle owns a house in a lovely *place* in the country.
   - a. land
   - b. location
   - c. atmosphere
   - d. downtown

IDIOMS

Find each idiom in the story and translate the sentences into Japanese.

1. (　　　)(　　　)(　　　)(　　　) = 一方

   The food at the restaurant was terrible. (　　　)(　　　)(　　　)(　　　), the coffee there was wonderful!

2. (　　　)(one's)(　　　) = （人の）注意を引く，（人の）目を引く

   While we were window shopping, this dress (　　　) my (　　　).（過去形で）

3. (　　　)(　　　)(　　　)(　　　)(　　　) = 実は

   Is she staying here long? No, (　　　)(　　　)(　　　)(　　　)(　　　), she is flying to Paris tomorrow.

Helping Others

慈善活動

困っている人々が世界中にたくさんいます。そのような人達に対し、どのような慈善活動が行われているか知っていますか。また、どのような人が寄付をするのでしょうか。その金額はいくらぐらいなのでしょうか。今回は慈善活動の実態について読んでみましょう。

TARGET VOCABULARY

Look up each word in a dictionary and match it with the closest meaning.

1. billion　　＿＿＿＿＿　(　) a. money or goods given to a charity
2. donation　＿＿＿＿＿　(　) b. thousand million
3. survey　　＿＿＿＿＿　(　) c. rich
4. volunteer　＿＿＿＿＿　(　) d. a way to do research by asking questions
5. wealthy　　＿＿＿＿＿　(　) e. work or help without being paid

READING PASSAGE

1   Giving time or taking time to help others is a common way that people give to others. In a **survey**, **Charities Aid Foundation** (CAF) asked thousands of people in over 150 countries about ways they gave to others in the month before the survey. The results showed that 45% of people worldwide took time to help a stranger in
5 some way. By contrast, about 20% of people who took the survey said they helped others by giving some of their time **volunteering** with groups.

   The CAF survey did not ask about how people gave things to others, but it is clear that giving things is quite common. People may buy extra food or other items in order to give these things to charities or to those in need. People may also give things they
10 do not need or use any longer, such as clothes, phones, or even an old car. These kinds of donations of new or used items actually add up to a lot of help for those who need it.

   When it came to giving money, the CAF survey found that over the past month, 33% of people had donated money. Over the years, the United States has been one of
15 the most generous countries worldwide. Each year, people, companies, and organizations in the United States donate over $300 **billion**. Actually, 75% of this amount, or over $225 billion, comes from people. Half of that is donated each year by average people and families and half is donated by richer people.

   Recently, the very rich have been challenged to give even more by the **Giving**
20 **Pledge**. A group of very **wealthy** people like Warren Buffet and Bill Gates started this idea. They want others to promise to donate most of their wealth now or at some point in the future. So far, over 50 billionaires around the world have joined Buffet and Gates in the Giving Pledge.

319 words

Notes 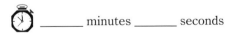 _____ minutes _____ seconds

Charities Aid Foundation「慈善活動支援協会」(1974年設立のイギリスの慈善団体.)　**Giving Pledge**「寄付の誓い」(Microsoft 会長のビル・ゲイツや資産家のウォーレン・バフェットが中心となり 2009 年に設立された．大富豪をターゲットとし彼らの資産の寄付を促す．賛同者は資産の寄付の約束をする．)

READING COMPREHENSION

Circle the letter of the best answer.

1. What is the best title for the passage?
   a. Money for Those In Need
   b. Ways to Give
   c. The Best Charities
   d. Why We Need Charities

2. What did the Charities Aid Foundation do?
   a. found volunteers for a group
   b. helped many strangers
   c. gave money to 150 countries
   d. surveyed people

3. According to research, how do most people "give to others"?
   a. They donate items to charities.
   b. They help strangers.
   c. They give money.
   d. They volunteer with organizations.

4. Where does over $225 billion in donations from the USA come from?
   a. from people
   b. from organizations
   c. from companies
   d. from rich people

5. Which of the following is NOT true about the Giving Pledge?
   a. People give most of their wealth when they join the pledge.
   b. Rich people worldwide have joined the Giving Pledge.
   c. The Giving Pledge is only for very wealthy people.
   d. Two billionaires who took the pledge are Warren Buffet and Bill Gates.

LISTENING COMPREHENSION 05

Listen to the CD and fill in the blanks.

The Charities Aid Foundation (CAF) gave a survey to thousands of people worldwide. In the survey, CAF asked people how they helped others or gave to those (1)_____ over the previous month. Most people said that they helped strangers, but others said they (2)_____ with groups to help others. The CAF survey did not ask about donating (3)_____ to charities or people, but it did ask about donating money. When it (4)_____ giving money, people seem very generous worldwide. One out of every three people said they had (5)_____ money over the previous month.

7

VOCABULARY REINFORCEMENT

Circle the letter of the best answer.

1. _____ reading in English, I like to be in a quiet room.
   a. All of a sudden
   b. By contrast
   c. Over time
   d. When it comes to

2. Martha _____ her brother to a game of basketball.
   a. challenged
   b. defined
   c. guided
   d. volunteered

3. Our class is studying for the school's math _____ next week.
   a. charity
   b. competition
   c. donation
   d. stranger

4. The World Food Programme is a famous international _____.
   a. amount
   b. month
   c. organization
   d. survey

5. Millions of people watched the _____ broadcast of the soccer game.
   a. generous
   b. in need
   c. wealthy
   d. worldwide

IDIOMS

Find each idiom in the story and translate the sentences into Japanese.

1. ( ) ( ) = 一方
   A glass of water has 0 calories. A glass of soda, ( ) ( ), has over 120 calories.

2. ( ) ( ) = 困っている
   Many families were ( ) ( ) after the flood.

3. ( ) ( ) ( ) ( ) = 〜に関して言えば
   ( ) ( ) ( ) ( ) making spaghetti, my father is better at it than my mother.

Movie Directors

女性映画監督

今も昔も娯楽の定番と言えば、映画ですね。世界中で映画祭が開催され、監督賞が毎年授与されますが、女性映画監督の受賞者は多いのでしょうか、それとも少ないのでしょうか。本文に出てくる映画を何本見たことがあるか数えてみたり、DVDを見たりするのもいいかもしれません。

TARGET VOCABULARY

Look up each word in a dictionary and match it with the closest meaning.

1. _____ animated ( ) a. a prize that honors the winner
2. _____ award ( ) b. a show that makes people laugh
3. _____ career ( ) c. ten years
4. _____ comedy ( ) d. years of working in one job
5. _____ decade ( ) e. drawn in a way to show movement; like a cartoon for a movie or TV

READING PASSAGE

1   Every year, major movie festivals around the world present **awards** for **Best Director**. Some of these festivals began **decades** ago, and their lists of winners for Best Director awards are quite long. However, among all the names of winners, it is hard to find the names of many female directors.

5   **The Cannes Film Festival** was the first major movie festival to name a female director as Best Director of the Year. In 1961, a Russian director named Yuliya Solntseva won at Cannes for her movie *Chronicle of Flaming Years*. Since then, no female director won Best Director at Cannes. Other women directed movies that won the *Palme d'Or* (Best Picture) at Cannes, but those female directors did not win the
10 Best Director award.

The Best Director award at the Berlin International Film Festival is called the **Silver Bear award**. Only one woman has succeeded in winning the Silver Bear. That woman was Astrid Henning-Jensen from Denmark. Over her **career**, Mrs. Henning-Jensen directed over 20 movies. In 1979, she won the Silver Bear for her movie
15 *Winterborn*.

One of the most difficult festivals for a female director to win Best Director at seems to be **the Academy Awards** (often called the Oscars) in the USA. In fact, since the Academy Awards began in 1929, only four women have ever been nominated for the Best Director award. The first woman to actually win this award was Kathryn
20 Bigelow (seen on the right in the picture on page 9) for directing *The Hurt Locker*. She received the award in 2010.

Over the years, women have directed lots of popular movies. For example, Nora Ephron directed the hit romantic-**comedy** *Sleepless in Seattle*, and Catherine Hardwicke directed the popular 2008 horror movie *Twilight*. Two very famous
25 **animated** movies were directed by a woman — Vicky Jenson directed *Shrek* in 2001 and *Shark Tale* in 2004.

310 words

Notes

Best Director「監督賞」 The Cannes Film Festival「カンヌ映画祭」(フランスのカンヌで毎年5月に開催される。) *Chronicle of Flaming Years* 映画『戦場』(ユリア・ソーンツェワ監督) Silver Bear award「銀熊賞」 *Palme d'Or*「パルムドール」(最優秀映画賞) *Winterborn* 映画『冬生まれの子ら』(アストリズ・ヘニング・イエンセン監督) the Academy Awards「アカデミー賞」(アメリカの映画賞。) *Sleepless in Seattle* 映画『めぐり逢えたら』(ノーラ・エフロン監督) *Twilight* 映画『トワイライト〜初恋〜』(キャサリン・ハードウィック監督) *Shrek* 映画『シュレック』(ビッキー・ジェンソン監督) *Shark Tale* 映画『シャーク・テイル』(ビッキー・ジェンソン監督)

READING COMPREHENSION

Circle the letter of the best answer.

1. What is the main topic of the passage?
   a. a problem female directors face
   b. the top award for female directors
   c. the most famous female director
   d. three women who directed great films
2. Which is true about the Cannes Film Festival?
   a. It began in 1961.
   b. It gives the Palme d'Or as the Best Director award.
   c. It has rarely recognized a woman as Best Director.
   d. It was not open to Russian directors before 1960.
3. What did Astrid Henning-Jensen do?
   a. began her movie career in Berlin
   b. spent two decades making *Winterborn*
   c. directed her first movie in 1979
   d. won the Silver Bear
4. How many women had won an Academy Award for Best Director before Kathryn Bigelow?
   a. none
   b. three
   c. four
   d. ten
5. What is probably true about the movies made by Nora Ephron, Catherine Hardwicke, and Vicky Jenson?
   a. They had more than one director.
   b. They were all romantic-comedies.
   c. They made a lot of money.
   d. They were nominated for Best Director awards.

LISTENING COMPREHENSION 07

Listen to the CD and fill in the blanks.

Very few female movie directors have succeeded in winning Best Director awards from (1)_____ international movie festivals. Before 2011, only one woman had been (2) _____ Best Director at each of the famous movie award festivals in France, Berlin, and the USA. Why is it so (3)_____ female directors in the lists of Best Director winners at these festivals? Some top female directors have been making movies for (4)_____! Furthermore, female directors have made all kinds of hit movies from romantic comedies to horror movies to animated movies. It is surprising that female directors have not won more (5)_____ for Best Director.

11

VOCABULARY REINFORCEMENT

Circle the letter of the word or phrase that best completes the sentence.

1. All of the teachers at the school were _____ until Mr. Brown started teaching there.
   a. comedy
   b. decade
   c. female
   d. silver

2. I _____ Judy as the leader of our group. She will do a great job!
   a. challenge
   b. nominate
   c. perform
   d. spin

3. James Cameron has directed many hit movies over his _____.
   a. award
   b. career
   c. donation
   d. festival

4. Many people think flowers, chocolate, and jewelry are _____ gifts.
   a. difficult
   b. international
   c. major
   d. romantic

5. My brother likes _____ movies more than movies with real actors in them.
   a. animated
   b. combined
   c. horror
   d. wealthy

IDIOMS

Find each idiom in the story and translate the sentences into Japanese.

1. (   ) (   ) (   ) (   ) = 見つけにくい，希少である

   The store (   ) not (   ) (   ) (   ). Just look for its big yellow sign.

2. (   ) (someone) (   ) = 〜として（人）の名を挙げる

   The judges (   ) my sister (   ) the best artist at this year's school art contest.（過去形で）

3. (   ) (   ) = 成功する

   Astronauts (   ) (   ) landing on the moon in 1969.（過去形で）

Around the World

世界一周

海外旅行をしたことがありますか。日本と異なる文化に触れ、現地の人々とコミュニケーションを取るのも旅の楽しみの1つですね。飛行機や船に乗って世界中の国に行けたらどんなに楽しいことでしょう。昔から様々なやり方で世界一周に挑戦する探検家がたくさんいました。彼らはどのように世界一周をし、どのくらいの時間をかけたのでしょうか。

TARGET VOCABULARY

Look up each word in a dictionary and match it with the closest meaning.

1. _____ article   (　) a. a person who goes to new places to learn about them
2. _____ author   (　) b. in the end; finally
3. _____ eventually   (　) c. a scientific idea
4. _____ explorer   (　) d. writer of books, articles, etc.
5. _____ theory   (　) e. newspaper or magazine story

READING PASSAGE

1   These days, we all know the world is round, but for most of human history, people thought it was flat. That is, they thought that if you traveled far enough in one direction, you would **eventually** come to the edge of the world. Then, about 2,000 years ago, people started to come up with the theory that the earth was round. This meant that by traveling far enough in a straight line, you would eventually come back to where you started.

   It was not until the 16th century that **Ferdinand Magellan's** expedition became the first to travel around the world. The expedition first sailed west from Portugal, around South America, and across the Pacific, before returning around South Africa to go back to Portugal. Even though Magellan died during the voyage, one of his captains, Juan Sebastian Elcano, made it all the way.

   In 1872, the French science fiction **author** Jules Verne published a book called *Around the World in 80 Days*. The novel was about a man who travels around the world, starting from London, to win a bet.

   In 1889, an American journalist, Nellie Bly, was sent by her newspaper to complete the journey taken by the characters in Verne's book. She traveled around the world by boat and train, sending **articles** back to her newspaper about her journey. She finally arrived back home after her trip, taking 72 days, six hours, and eleven minutes to go around the world.

   As air travel made a trip around the world a little easier and much faster, people used planes or other aircraft for record-making trips around the world. The first airplane flight around the world took place in 1924, completed by **Lt.** Lowell H. Smith and five other American pilots, and the first solo helicopter flight around the world was done by an Australian **explorer**, Dick Smith, in 1982-83. As for a nonstop balloon flight all the way around the world, this was not completed until 2002, when Steve Fossett eventually succeeded on his sixth attempt.

   However, some people take their time. Dave Kunst took from 1970 to 1974 to become the first person to walk all the way around the world. The American wore out 21 pairs of shoes on his trip!

374 words

Notes   _____ minutes _____ seconds

Ferdinand Magellan「フェルディナンド・マゼラン」(ポルトガルの探検家.) *Around the World in 80 Days* 小説『80日間世界一周』(ジュール・ヴェルヌ作) **Lt.**「米陸軍中尉」

READING COMPREHENSION

Circle the letter of the best answer.

1. What is the main topic of the passage?
   a. how people moved from country to country
   b. a famous book about travel
   c. why people prefer planes to boats
   d. people who travel around the world

2. Who first said that the world was not flat?
   a. Ferdinand Magellan
   b. Jules Verne
   c. Nellie Bly
   d. The passage does not say.

3. Which of these people did NOT go on a journey around the world?
   a. Ferdinand Magellan
   b. Jules Verne
   c. Nellie Bly
   d. Steve Fossett

4. What did Jules Verne and Nellie Bly have in common?
   a. They both traveled around the world.
   b. They were both American.
   c. They both wrote about traveling around the world.
   d. They were both journalists.

5. Which of these people did NOT travel around the world by air?
   a. Nellie Bly
   b. Lowell H. Smith
   c. Dick Smith
   d. Steve Fossett

LISTENING COMPREHENSION   09

Listen to the CD and fill in the blanks.

(1)_____ it's very easy to travel around the world, but it wasn't always like this. The first expedition to go all the way around the world was led by the (2)_____ Ferdinand Magellan, in the 16th century. (3)_____ you can easily fly around the world now, people are still interested in breaking records. One man walked around the world. His trip took four years before he (4) _____ finished, and he (5)_____ 21 pairs of shoes!

VOCABULARY REINFORCEMENT

Circle the letter of the word or phrase that best completes the sentence.

1. I read a great _____ in the newspaper this morning.
   a. article
   b. novel
   c. journalist
   d. author

2. I waited for about 30 minutes before the bus _____ came.
   a. explorer
   b. reported
   c. eventually
   d. in addition

3. Have a great _____! See you next week.
   a. explorer
   b. trip
   c. theory
   d. novel

4. She has a very interesting _____ about what happened to the dinosaurs.
   a. explorer
   b. journalist
   c. location
   d. theory

5. After I graduate, I'd like to get a job as a(n) _____ on a newspaper.
   a. journalist
   b. author
   c. article
   d. program

IDIOMS

Find each idiom in the story and translate the sentences into Japanese.

1. (   ) (   ) = この頃
   People have no manners (   ) (   ).

2. (   ) (   ) = 〜にもかかわらず，たとえ〜でも
   I passed the exam, (   ) (   ) I didn't study.

3. (   ) (   ) = 着古す，使い古す
   Mary jogs so often that she (   ) (   ) her shoes in just a few weeks.

Yuna Kim
キム・ヨナ

冬の人気のスポーツと言えば、あなたはどのスポーツを思い浮かべますか。今回は大人気のフィギュアスケートとその代表的な選手であるキム・ヨナの話です。キム・ヨナは浅田真央のライバルで大きな大会でお互い切磋琢磨していました。キム・ヨナは世界記録をいくつか樹立しましたが、その得点は何点だったのでしょうか。

TARGET VOCABULARY

Look up each word in a dictionary and match it with the closest meaning.

1. _____ combined   ( ) a. but, apart from
2. _____ element   ( ) b. part of something
3. _____ except   ( ) c. do; act, dance, etc. in front of people
4. _____ perform   ( ) d. a well-developed talent
5. _____ skill   ( ) e. put together; added to each other

READING PASSAGE

1   Yuna Kim is one of the world's best figure skaters. At the **2010 Winter Olympics in Vancouver**, she set three world records. In fact, one of those world records broke a record she set in 2009.

   At the Olympics, both male and female skaters **perform** a **short program** and a
5 **long program**. In the short program, skaters have less than three minutes to perform seven required jumps, spins, or other moves. While doing these seven things, the skaters also have to show judges how well they can put these **elements** together into a kind of dance performance on the ice. The long program is **similar** to the short program **except** that skaters perform for a longer time and have more required
10 moves.

   Before the 2010 Winter Olympics began, many people thought Yuna Kim was likely to win a gold medal. Certainly, there were other women skaters who had the **skill** to win gold at the Olympics. However, Ms. Kim had an advantage. She had already set a number of world records. In 2007, she set the record for the highest score in a short
15 program with 71.95 points in Japan. The same year she also set the world record for the highest score in a long program with 133.7 points in Russia. Then, in 2009 she beat her own record in the short program by scoring 76.12 in the United States. At that competition, she also became the first woman to score over 200 points with her short and long programs — her **combined** score was 207.71.

20 The next year at the Winter Olympics in Vancouver, she broke her records again. In the short program, Ms. Kim scored 78.5, a new world record. In the long program, she scored 150.06, another world record. This gave her a combined total of 228.56 points, a third world record! Needless to say, her score was enough to win gold.

315 words

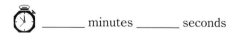 _____ minutes _____ seconds

Notes

short program「ショートプログラム」　long program「フリープログラム（ロングプログラムまたはフリースケーティング）」　2010 Winter Olympics in Vancouver「2010年バンクーバー冬季オリンピック」（カナダのバンクーバーで2010年2月12日から2月28日に行われた．）　similar「似ている」　except「～を除いて」

READING COMPREHENSION

Circle the letter of the best answer.

1. What is the best title for the passage?
   a. A Woman with Many World Records
   b. The Winter Olympics
   c. Short and Long Programs in Figure Skating
   d. Two Years on Ice

2. How long should an Olympic figure skater's short program be?
   a. shorter than 2 minutes
   b. under 3 minutes
   c. about 7 minutes
   d. between 3 and 7 minutes

3. What is true about Ms. Kim's score in the long program at the US competition in 2009?
   a. It was just under 72 points.
   b. It was about 76 points.
   c. It was over 123 points.
   d. It was above 200 points.

4. Which of Ms. Kim's scores set a world record at the 2010 Winter Olympics?
   a. her score in the short program
   b. her combined score for the short and long programs
   c. her score in the long program
   d. all of the above

5. What did Yuna Kim NOT do at the 2010 Winter Olympics?
   a. break one of her own world records
   b. skate in a long program for the first time
   c. set world records
   d. win a gold medal

LISTENING COMPREHENSION

 11

Listen to the CD and fill in the blanks.

In the 2010 Winter Olympics, Yuna Kim (1)_____ three world records! For the Olympics, figure skaters must (2) _____ short programs and long programs. Both kinds of programs have required elements such as (3)_____ and jumps that judges watch. Along with these skating skills, figure skaters must create a performance that is (4)_____ a dance. Needless to say, Yuna Kim did this very well when she set her world records. She not only won the gold medal at the Winter Olympics, but she also got a (5)_____ score of 228.56 points for her short and long programs!

VOCABULARY REINFORCEMENT

Circle the letter of the best answer.

Circle the letter of the word or phrase that best matches the word(s) in *italics*.

1. We *put together* our money so that we could buy the book.
   - a. combined
   - b. highest
   - c. required
   - d. wealthy
2. I like all kinds of fruit *but* bananas.
   - a. already
   - b. except
   - c. instead
   - d. probably
3. Ms. Tan's score was too high. No other athlete could *compete* with her.
   - a. challenge
   - b. perform
   - c. spin
   - d. volunteer
4. The *people giving points* enjoyed the dancer's performance. They all gave her high scores.
   - a. elements
   - b. judges
   - c. medals
   - d. skills
5. Your bicycle *is like* my bicycle.
   - a. is similar to
   - b. breaks a record
   - c. shows the way
   - d. takes part in

IDIOMS

Find each idiom in the story and translate the sentences into Japanese.

1. (   ) (   ) (   ) = 記録を打ち立てる

   She tried to (   ) (   ) world (   ) by not sleeping for two weeks, but she could not do it.

2. (   ) (   ) (   ) = 〜と似ている

   The two stories (   ) (   ) (   ) to each other, but they were not exactly the same. （過去形で）

3. (   ) (   ) (   ) = 言うまでもなく

   His score on the test was lower than he expected. (   ) (   ) (   ), he was disappointed.

The Puffer Fish

フグの毒にご注意

上の写真を見て、この奇妙な形をした魚が何の魚かわかりますか。そうです、フグです。フグは日本では高級魚として知られていて、刺身、鍋、唐揚げもおいしい魚です。でも実は危険な毒を持つ魚で、フグを食べた後、重症で入院あるいは亡くなってしまう人もいます。フグの有毒な部分を食べてしまうとどういう症状が出るのでしょうか。

TARGET VOCABULARY

Look up each word in a dictionary and match it with the closest meaning.

1. _____ breathe   ( ) a. something that hurts or kills people if they eat or touch it
2. _____ identify   ( ) b. take air into and out of the body
3. _____ poison   ( ) c. a sign of a sickness or disease
4. _____ remove   ( ) d. show or find out who someone is or what
5. _____ symptom   ( ) e. take away

READING PASSAGE

1   When three men in California were taken to a hospital with strange **symptoms**, the hospital doctors thought the men had been **poisoned**. They felt dizzy, tired, and weak. The men couldn't speak, and they had trouble **breathing**. The doctors couldn't work out what was wrong with the men until they found out the three men were all chefs, and they had just shared a dish of *fugu*.

Fugu, the Japanese name for the **puffer fish**, is one of the strangest fish in the ocean. The puffer fish gets its name from the way the fish protects itself from enemies. Whenever it is attacked, the fish **puffs up** (blows up) its body to **over twice its normal size**!

The reason the three men were taken to the hospital is because the puffer fish is also very **poisonous**. As a rule, if you eat a whole puffer fish, you will probably die. The three men **had a close call**, but they all survived.

The symptoms of fugu poisoning are a strange feeling around the mouth and throat, and difficulty breathing. You can't breathe, and your body can't get any air. Your brain still works perfectly, however, so you know you are dying, but you can't speak or do anything about it.

Despite the danger of fugu poisoning, this strange, ugly, and very poisonous fish is actually a very expensive, and very popular, kind of food in Japan. Customers pay up to $200 per person to eat a fugu meal. Because of the danger, fugu can only be prepared by chefs with **a special license** from the government. These chefs are trained to **identify** and **remove** the poisonous parts of the fish. Most people who die from eating fugu these days are people who have tried their hand at preparing the fish themselves.

Fugu is said to be so delicious that it has even started to be imported into Hong Kong and the United States. Several tons of fugu are now exported from Japan every year.

333 words

Notes  _____ minutes _____ seconds

puffer fish「フグ」（blowfish とも言う）　**puff up**「膨らませる」　**over twice its normal size**「通常の大きさの2倍以上」　**poisonous**「有毒な」　**have a close call**「危機一髪のところで助かる」　**special license**「特別な免許」（本文では「フグ処理師免許」を指す。）

READING COMPREHENSION

Circle the letter of the best answer.

1. What is the best title for the passage?
   a. Fishing in Japan
   b. A Dangerous Dish
   c. The History of Fugu
   d. A Talented Chef

2. Why were the three men taken to the hospital?
   a. Someone poisoned them.
   b. They ate poison by accident.
   c. They poisoned each other.
   d. A doctor worked out their symptoms.

3. What does the puffer fish do when an enemy tries to eat it?
   a. It eats the enemy.
   b. It makes poison.
   c. It looks very ugly.
   d. It becomes bigger.

4. What is NOT a symptom of fugu poisoning?
   a. breathing difficulty
   b. tiredness and weakness
   c. trouble speaking
   d. your brain stops working

5. According to the passage, who is allowed to serve fugu?
   a. people from California
   b. licensed chefs
   c. the government
   d. anyone who wants to try their hand

LISTENING COMPREHENSION   13

Listen to the CD and fill in the blanks.

The puffer fish has a natural (1) _____ in its body. When people eat fugu that hasn't been prepared carefully, they show several strange (2)_____. The person's mouth and throat feel funny, they can't (3) _____ , and they can't move. As a rule, people should not (4)_____ serving this food at home. People should only eat fugu if it is served by a chef with a special (5)_____.

23

VOCABULARY REINFORCEMENT

Circle the letter of the word or phrase that best matches the words in *italics*.

1. The United States *brings in* most of the oil it uses from Canada.
    a. exports
    b. imports
    c. removes
    d. breathes

2. One of the *signs* of a cold is often a high temperature.
    a. licenses
    b. theories
    c. poisons
    d. symptoms

3. Australia *sells* a lot of beef to countries in Asia.
    a. exports
    b. imports
    c. licenses
    d. hires

4. A tree fell over in my garden, so I called someone to *take it away*.
    a. identify it
    b. create it
    c. remove it
    d. roast it

5. Cathy does not use the computer for more than an hour each night *usually*.
    a. as a rule
    b. close call
    c. needless to say
    d. trying her hand

IDIOMS

Find each idiom in the story and translate the sentences into Japanese.

1. (　　　) (　　　) (　　　) = 普通
   (　　　) (　　　) (　　　), I don't drink coffee before I go to bed.

2. (　　　) (　　　) (　　　) = 危機一髪
   I had (　　　) (　　　) (　　　) when my car crashed.

3. (　　　) one's (　　　) (　　　) something = 初めて試す
   On my vacation, I (　　　) my (　　　) (　　　) scuba diving.（過去形で）

Technology in the Classroom

教室でコンピューターを使おう

スマートフォンやタブレットやノートパソコンなどの機器を電車やバスで使う人をよく見かけます。それらは本当に便利で、なくてはならない存在になっています。学校の授業でもそういった機器を活用するようになりました。だからと言って、授業中に私用でスマートフォンを使うのはダメですね。ほら、先生が怖い顔をしてにらんでいますよ。

TARGET VOCABULARY

Look up each word in a dictionary and match it with the closest meaning.

1. _____ access   (   ) a. be able to buy
2. _____ afford   (   ) b. creation; design and production
3. _____ development   (   ) c. get into; able to use
4. _____ organized   (   ) d. machines or devices that make life easier
5. _____ technology   (   ) e. well-planned; arranged

READING PASSAGE

1   Many classrooms today have computers in them. However, there are usually not enough for each student to use one at the same time. Computers cost a lot and they also use space in small classrooms. **Laptop computers** are more convenient because they need less space and they can be carried or moved easily. However, most schools
5 still cannot **afford** enough computers for all of the students to have one.

   Since the **development** of the first computer, these machines have continued to become smaller, lighter, and cheaper. These days there are cheaper devices that are small enough to be held in one hand but are still very powerful. The development of these **handheld devices** is allowing more schools to bring **technology** into
10 classrooms.

   Some of the first handheld devices were called **PDA**s, personal digital assistants. They were used to help people in business stay **organized**. They could make lists of things to do each day, **store** important phone numbers, and even make files for work. Now we have smart phones and small tablet computers. The latest devices have come
15 a long way since those early PDA models. Those used in schools today can do all the things PDAs did and more! They can access the Internet, play games, and run useful programs, for example, those that help in science experiments.

   Because handheld devices are relatively cheap, schools can afford to buy more of them. In some schools, students pay a **deposit** at the beginning of the year for a
20 handheld device. Since the students paid a deposit, they tend to take better care of the device over the year. The students can get the deposit back at the end of the year if they return the device in good condition. Or, students can just pay a little more money to keep it at the end of the year.

   In the future, schools might be able to afford computers or laptops for every student.
25 Until then, handheld devices are turning out to be good things to use instead.

                                                                              336 words

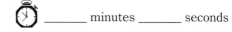 _____ minutes _____ seconds

laptop computer「ノートパソコン」 **PDA**「携帯情報端末」(アップルコンピュータ CEO のジョン・スカリーによる造語.) **handheld device**「携帯機器」 **store**「保存する」 **have come a long way**「大きな進歩を遂げた」 **deposit**「保証金」

READING COMPREHENSION

Circle the letter of the best answer.

1. What is the best title for the passage?
   a. Computer Programs for Students
   b. Students Need More Computers
   c. Handhelds Help Schools
   d. Studying Technology
2. Why do schools not have enough computers for students?
   a. Computer programs are not useful.
   b. Handhelds do not work with computers.
   c. Computers are expensive.
   d. Most students have their own laptops.
3. Which of the following is NOT true about handheld devices?
   a. Most laptops are cheaper than handhelds.
   b. Students can use them to email files to each other.
   c. Schools can afford to buy many of them.
   d. They were first developed for business people.
4. What do some students pay a deposit for?
   a. to access the Internet for one year
   b. to do science experiments
   c. to return a device in good condition
   d. to use one of the school's devices
5. Which statement would the writer probably agree with?
   a. All students need to learn to write programs.
   b. Handheld devices are useful for students.
   c. Schools should teach more computer classes.
   d. Technology can make classes more difficult.

LISTENING COMPREHENSION 15

Listen to the CD and fill in the blanks.

Computers are not cheap devices. Schools cannot (1) _____ lots of them for students to use in classrooms. However, technology has come a long way since the early days of computers. These days, handheld devices can do many things similar to computers. Students can (2) _____ the Internet, run programs, and make schedules to keep their classes and homework (3) _____ . Best of all, these devices are much cheaper than computers! Handheld devices are (4)_____ to be a great choice for schools that want to bring (5)_____ into the classroom for all students to use.

27

VOCABULARY REINFORCEMENT

Circle the letter of the best answer.

1. The shoes cost less than $10. That seems _____ to me.
   a. casual
   b. cheap
   c. major
   d. organized

2. All of the pictures that I took at our picnic _____ very nice. I will make copies of them for you.
   a. came a long way
   b. tended to be
   c. turned out
   d. tried my hand at

3. My computer is old, so many of the newest _____ won't run on it.
   a. articles
   b. models
   c. programs
   d. symptoms

4. Only people who work in the store can _____ the storage room.
   a. access
   b. afford
   c. export
   d. remove

5. The spider's bite has a little _____ in it, but it will not hurt a person
   a. license
   b. development
   c. poison
   d. technology

IDIOMS

Find each idiom in the story and translate the sentences into Japanese.

1. (　　　) (　　　) (　　　) (　　　) = 大きな進歩を遂げる

   With the help of her tutor, her writing skills have (　　　) (　　　) (　　　) (　　　).（過去分詞形で）

   _____

2. (　　　) (　　　) = ～する傾向がある

   Students who learn to play music (　　　) (　　　) do better in math.

   _____

3. (　　　) (　　　) = ～であることがわかる，結果的に～になる

   I thought the swimming class would be boring, but it (　　　) (　　　) to be a lot of fun.（過去形で）

   _____

Interesting Buildings

変わった建物

世の中には変わった形をした建物がたくさんあります。その形状を見れば、その建物が何に関連しているのかがわかるようにデザインされた外観になっているものもあります。世界にはどのような形をした建物があるか想像してみてください。犬や猫の形をしたペットショップはたくさんありそうですね。

TARGET VOCABULARY

Look up each word in a dictionary and match it with the closest meaning.

1. _____ giant ( ) a. bring to mind something from the past
2. _____ imagination ( ) b. see again and know what/who it is
3. _____ recognize ( ) c. very large; huge
4. _____ remind ( ) d. something used to help make or build other things
5. _____ tool ( ) e. the ability to see or make things with one's mind

READING PASSAGE

1   There are some famous buildings that everyone can **recognize**. When you see a picture of a sports stadium that **reminds** you of a bird's nest, you probably know it is the Olympic stadium in Beijing. When you see a picture of a famous concert hall that reminds you of a sailing ship, you probably know it is **the Sydney Opera House** in
5   Australia. Buildings like these are easily recognized worldwide. They were designed to look like other things if people use their **imaginations**.

Other buildings do not need any imagination. They are made to look exactly like other things. Sometimes, these buildings are offices, restaurants, or even houses. Three buildings built in this way are actually museums. The shape of the building is a
10   clue to the objects people can see inside.

In **Guizhou**, China, people can visit **the Meitan Tea Museum**, built in the shape of a **giant** teapot. There is also a second building next door that is shaped like a tea cup. From far away, the **nine-story teapot-shaped** museum looks like some kind of giant work of art. But as one gets closer, the windows make it clear that this is a
15   building.

People who are interested in guitars might want to visit the Guitar Museum in Tennessee, USA. The three-story building is shaped like a guitar **lying on its side**. Inside, visitors can see all kinds of guitars as well as learn about famous guitar players.

One of the newest funny-shaped museums is a pottery museum in **Gyeonggi**,
20   Korea. This museum, built in 2011, is shaped just like a traditional Korean pot. Along with seeing examples of pots and tools used for making pots in the museum, visitors can try to make their own pots there.

290 words

the Sydney Opera House「シドニー・オペラハウス」 Guizhou「貴州」(中国の省の1つ.) the Meitan Tea Museum「湄潭（びたん）紅茶博物館」 nine-story teapot-shaped「9階建てのティーポット型の」 lying on its side「横倒しの」 Gyeonggi「京畿（道）」(韓国の行政区)

READING COMPREHENSION

Circle the letter of the best answer.

1. What is the main topic of the passage?
   a. famous things from long ago
   b. interesting buildings
   c. famous museums
   d. things used to make buildings

2. What are the stadium and the concert hall examples of?
   a. famous buildings in Beijing
   b. buildings that look exactly like things in them
   c. giant buildings
   d. places that look like other things

3. Where can people visit a building that looks like a teapot?
   a. in Australia
   b. in Korea
   c. in China
   d. in the USA

4. What is NOT true about the building that looks like a guitar?
   a. People can see guitars inside of it.
   b. You can find information about famous guitar players there.
   c. It is in Tennessee.
   d. The two-story building is shaped like a guitar lying on its side.

5. Which is probably true about people who work in the teapot-shaped museum?
   a. They make tools.
   b. They put food in the pots in the building.
   c. They opened the building a decade ago.
   d. They teach people how to make pots.

LISTENING COMPREHENSION 17

Listen to the CD and fill in the blanks.

Sometimes buildings are built to look like other things. For example, a (1)_____ in Beijing is similar in shape to a bird's nest. And a concert hall in Sydney might (2)_____ you of a sailing ship if you use your imagination. Then there are other buildings that are (3)_____ to look just like certain things. You would be sure to (4)_____ the Meitan Tea Museum in China. It looks like a teapot with a tea cup next to it. There are also a guitar museum in the USA that looks just like a guitar and a pottery museum in Korea that looks like a (5)_____ traditional Korean pot!

VOCABULARY REINFORCEMENT

Circle the letter of the word or phrase that best matches the words in *italics*.

1. That is not my father's car. It just *is similar to* his car.
   - a. looks like
   - b. makes it clear
   - c. tends to
   - d. turns out

2. If you like to *create* clothes, you should consider a career in fashion.
   - a. access
   - b. design
   - c. recognize
   - d. remind

3. The restaurant makes *huge* hamburgers. One person cannot eat a whole one.
   - a. cheap
   - b. shaped
   - c. horror
   - d. giant

4. The city will build a new *place for sports* to host the World Cup soccer competition.
   - a. guitar
   - b. pottery
   - c. stadium
   - d. tool

5. There were a lot of people at the *show*. The band is more popular than I thought.
   - a. concert
   - b. imagination
   - c. model
   - d. technology

IDIOMS

Find each idiom in the story and translate the sentences into Japanese.

1. (   ) (   ) = 〜のようにみえる

   His coat (   ) (   ) his father's coat, except his father's coat was bigger.（過去形で）

2. (   ) (   ) = 〜の隣に

   My best friend lives (   ) (   ) to me.

3. (   ) (   ) (   ) = 〜ということを示す，説明する

   The sound the dog is making and the way it is moving (   ) (   ) (   ) that it is hurt.

Bollywood

新映画の都　ボリウッド

ボリウッドという言葉を聞いたことがありますか。ほとんどの人が聞いたことがないと思います。どうやら映画の都・ハリウッドと関係がありそうです。写真に写っている人達もボリウッドの関係者です。ボリウッドはある国の映画産業を指します。まだ、見当がつかないですか。では本文を読んでみましょう。

TARGET VOCABULARY

Look up each word in a dictionary and match it with the closest meaning.

1. _____ shoot (a film)　( )　a. all businesses that make or sell a product
2. _____ compare　　　( )　b. see how two things are the same or different
3. _____ script　　　　( )　c. take pictures with a movie camera
4. _____ industry　　　( )　d. in a film, the background behind an actor or actress
5. _____ scenery　　　( )　e. the words that the actors in a film say

READING PASSAGE

1　Most people think that the capital of the movie world is **Hollywood**, in the United States. However, the real movie capital is **Mumbai**, in India. Mumbai used to be known as Bombay, and the movie **industry** there is often called "**Bollywood**." Bollywood makes twice as many movies each year as Hollywood — more than 1,000 movies a year.

　　The movies from Bollywood are very different from those made by Hollywood studios. For one thing, Bollywood movies are much longer than most Hollywood movies. Most Bollywood movies are more than three hours long, and contain singing, dancing, action, adventure, mystery, and romance (but usually no kissing). Because Bollywood movies contain so many different features, this style of movie is sometimes called a "**masala**" movie — "masala" is an Indian word for a mixture of spices.

　　Another big difference between Bollywood and Hollywood movies is the way the movies are made. It takes much longer to make a movie in Hollywood than in Bollywood. In fact, filming may begin on a Bollywood movie before the **script** is even finished. The director and writers can make up the story while the movie is being made. Sometimes they will even write the script by hand instead of taking time to type it.

　　Bollywood actors are very popular and some are in such high demand that they may work on several movies at the same time. They may even **shoot** scenes for several movies on the same day using the same costumes and **scenery**. Since most Bollywood movies follow the same kind of story, shooting scenes for several movies at the same time is not a big problem for actors or directors. This also helps keep the cost of Bollywood movies lower than the cost of Hollywood movies. The average Bollywood movie, with a budget of about two million U.S. dollars, seems very cheap **compared** to the average budget of nearly 70 million U.S. dollars for a Hollywood movie!

323 words

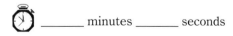

Notes

Hollywood「ハリウッド」(アメリカのロサンゼルスにあり,映画制作で有名.)　Mumbai「ムンバイ」(インドの都市ボンベイの正式名称で商工が盛んな港湾都市.)　Bollywood「ボリウッド」(ムンバイの映画産業を指す.ムンバイの旧称ボンベイとハリウッドを合わせた造語.)　masala「マサラ」(いろいろな香辛料を調合した調味料.)

READING COMPREHENSION

Circle the letter of the best answer.

1. What is the main topic of the passage?
   a. Famous stars in Bollywood
   b. The differences between two movie industries
   c. How Hollywood movies are made
   d. The history of movie-making in India

2. What is NOT true about Mumbai?
   a. It is the movie capital of India.
   b. More movies are made there than in Hollywood.
   c. The new name is Bombay.
   d. It is less expensive to make movies there than in Hollywood.

3. Why are Bollywood movies often called "masala" movies?
   a. They have spicy stories.
   b. They are much longer than Hollywood movies.
   c. They show Indian culture.
   d. They mix features from different styles of movies.

4. One of the reasons Bollywood movies are cheap to make is . . .
   a. they are shorter than Hollywood movies.
   b. the scripts are written by hand.
   c. the movies do not use any special effects.
   d. some movies reuse things from other movies.

5. Which statement would the writer probably agree with?
   a. Hollywood movies are too violent.
   b. It takes a lot of money to make a good movie.
   c. Most Bollywood movies are very similar.
   d. Only Indian people can understand Bollywood movies.

LISTENING COMPREHENSION   19

Listen to the CD and fill in the blanks.

Bollywood is the name of the movie (1)_____ in India. Bollywood moviemakers actually (2) _____ twice as many movies each year as moviemakers in Hollywood. If you (3) _____ the movies of the two industries, you can see several differences. (4) _____ , Bollywood movies are much longer than the average Hollywood movie. In addition, Bollywood movies reuse scenery and (5)_____ to keep the cost of the movies low.

VOCABULARY REINFORCEMENT

Circle the letter of the word or phrase that best completes the sentence

1. The director wants to _____ his new adventure movie in the jungle.
   a. arrange
   b. contain
   c. shoot
   d. create

2. The writer changed the movie's _____ five times.
   a. article
   b. material
   c. novel
   d. script

3. The photocopier was broken, so she copied the class notes _____.
   a. by hand
   b. for good
   c. on the other hand
   d. in high demand

4. If you _____ the phones carefully, you can tell this one is the best.
   a. license
   b. compare
   c. arrange
   d. decrease

5. People in the movie _____ can earn a lot of money.
   a. scenery
   b. costume
   c. industry
   d. mystery

IDIOMS

Find each idiom in the story and translate the sentences into Japanese.

1. (   ) (   ) (   ) = ひとつには
   I don't like him. (   ) (   ) (   ), he's always late.

2. (   ) (   ) = 自分の手で，機械を使わず
   I can type much faster than I can write (   ) (   ).

3. (   ) (high) (   ) = （大いに）求められている，需要がある
   The book was (   ) high (   ), and the bookstores sold out very quickly.

The Nobel Prize

ノーベル賞

年末になると誰がノーベル賞を取るのか大きな話題になります。皆さんはノーベル賞を受賞した日本人の名前を何人挙げることができますか。ノーベル賞はいくつかの部門に分かれていますが、どのような部門があるか知っていますか。将来、ノーベル賞の授賞者になれるよう、自分の得意な分野を磨いてみてはいかがですか。

TARGET VOCABULARY

Look up each word in a dictionary and match it with the closest meaning.

1. _____ aim ( ) a. one person
2. _____ individual ( ) b. start a building or organization
3. _____ annual ( ) c. happening every year
4. _____ (to) found (something) ( ) d. a material used to blow up things
5. _____ explosive ( ) e. purpose; goal

READING PASSAGE

1   Each year on December 10, the world's attention turns to Sweden for the announcement of the Nobel Prize winners. The Nobel Prizes, six prizes given to groups or **individuals** who really stand out in their fields, were **founded** by a Swedish inventor, **Alfred Nobel**.

5   Alfred Nobel was the man who invented dynamite, a powerful **explosive**. During his life, Nobel made a lot of money from his invention, and he decided that he wanted to use his money to help scientists, artists, and people who worked to help others around the world. When he died, his will said that the money would be placed in a bank, and the interest the money earned would be given out as five **annual** cash
10 prizes.

The prizes set up by Nobel were first handed out in 1901, and include prizes in physics, medicine, chemistry, literature, and peace. Later, in 1968 the Bank of Sweden added a prize in economics to celebrate the bank's 300th year of business.

Each person who receives a Nobel Prize is given a cash prize, a medal, and a
15 certificate. The prize money for each category is currently worth about 1.5 million dollars, and the **aim** of the prize is to allow the winner to carry on working or researching without having to worry about raising money.

The prizes can be given to either individuals or groups. Prize winners include **Albert Einstein** (physics, 1921), **Kim Dae Jung** (peace, 2000), **the United Nations**
20 (peace, 2001), **Barack Obama** (peace, 2009), and **Mario Vargas Llosa** (literature, 2010).

The prize winner that has won the most times is **the International Committee of the Red** Cross. This organization has received three Nobel Peace Prizes (in 1917, 1944, and 1963), and the founder, **Jean Henri Dunant**, was awarded the first Nobel
25 Peace Prize, in 1901.

299 words

Alfred Nobel「アルフレッド・ノーベル」(スウェーデンの化学者．ノーベル賞の設立者．) Albert Einstein「アルバート・アインシュタイン」(アメリカの理論物理学者．) Kim Dae Jung「金大中」(韓国の元大統領．)   the United Nations「国際連合」 Barack Obama「バラク・オバマ」(アメリカの大統領．)   Mario Vargas Llosa「マリオ・バルガス・リョサ」(ペルーの小説家．)   the International Committee of the Red Cross「赤十字国際委員会」 Jean Henri Dunant「ジャン・アンリ・デュナン」(赤十字社を創設した．)

READING COMPREHENSION

Circle the letter of the best answer.

1. What is the best title for the passage?
   a. The History of the Nobel Prize
   b. The Nobel Peace Prize
   c. How to Win a Nobel Prize
   d. Famous International Prizes

2. How did Alfred Nobel become rich?
   a. by winning a Nobel Prize
   b. through his inventions
   c. through the interest on his savings
   d. by receiving money from the Bank of Sweden

3. How many categories of Nobel Prize did Alfred Nobel create?
   a. one
   b. five
   c. six
   d. The passage does not say.

4. What statement about the Nobel Prizes is NOT true?
   a. They are given out every year.
   b. They can't be given to the same winner more than once.
   c. They are worth more than a million dollars each.
   d. They are given to both individuals and groups.

5. Who or what was the first Nobel Peace Prize Winner?
   a. Alfred Nobel
   b. Albert Einstein
   c. Jean Henri Dunant
   d. The International Committee of the Red Cross

LISTENING COMPREHENSION 21

Listen to the CD and fill in the blanks.

The Nobel Prizes are awards (1)_____ by Alfred Nobel. This inventor got rich from making dynamite, an (2)_____. Some of Nobel's money is still in the bank, and (3)_____ from this money is given to the winners of the Nobel Prizes. The (4)_____ of the prizes is to allow people to work or research without worrying about money. There are six (5) _____ of prizes: physics, medicine, chemistry, literature, peace, and economics.

VOCABULARY REINFORCEMENT

Circle the letter of the word or phrase that best matches the words in *italics*.

1. The students *continued* talking, even though their teacher was waiting for silence.
   a. ruled out
   b. wore out
   c. carried on
   d. stood out

2. Harvey listened for the *spoken message* to tell him the train was arriving at his station.
   a. announcement
   b. explosive
   c. category
   d. script

3. Every August I go to the town's *yearly* festival.
   a. complicated
   b. individual
   c. annual
   d. estimated

4. On the wall of the bank there is a portrait of the man who *started* it.
   a. announced
   b. remained
   c. poisoned
   d. founded

5. Groups of people usually take longer to make a decision than *one person*.
   a. individuals
   b. costumes
   c. baskets
   d. categories

IDIOMS

Find each idiom in the story and translate the sentences into Japanese.

1. (   ) (   ) = 目立つ

   Mary (   ) (   ) from the rest of her class by getting the highest score on every test.（過去形で）

2. (   ) (   ) = はじめる

   The bank teller helped me (   ) (   ) my new bank account.

3. (   ) (   ) = 続ける，続く

   Sorry for disturbing you. (   ) (   ) with what you were doing.

A Funny Cure

笑って治そう

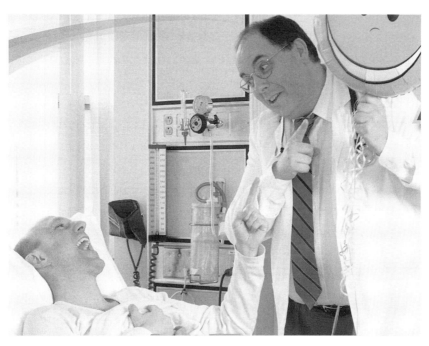

写真のような病院に入院したら楽しそうですね。昨日、何回笑ったか覚えていますか。人は楽しいと感じたときに笑います。笑うことが自分の体に何らかのよい影響を与えると言われたら、あなたは信じますか。今回は、医者から不治の病と言われた自分の病気を笑うことで治そうとした人の話です。

TARGET VOCABULARY

Look up each word in a dictionary and match it with the closest meaning.

1. _____ amusing ( ) a. medicine or treatment that makes a sick person healthy again
2. _____ cure ( ) b. (noun) a scientific test; (verb) test scientifically
3. _____ disease ( ) c. a sickness or serious illness
4. _____ painful ( ) d. funny
5. _____ experiment ( ) e. hurting

READING PASSAGE

1   There is an old English **saying**, "**Laughter** is the best medicine." One person who certainly would have agreed with this is Norman Cousins. Norman Cousins was the **editor** of a magazine called *Saturday Review* for almost 40 years. He also wrote and spoke about **world peace and anti-nuclear and anti-war issues,** traveling to many
5   different countries to share his ideas.

   In the 1960s, after returning to the United States from a busy and tiring trip to Europe, Mr. Cousins got sick. He discovered he had a rare **disease** known as **ankylosing spondylitis** that caused the joints between his bones to become stiff. In less than a week after he got back, he could not stand. Every move that he made was
10 **painful**. He was not able to sleep at night. The doctors told Mr. Cousins that they did not know how to **cure** his problem and he might never get over the illness. Mr. Cousins, however, refused to give up hope.

   Mr. Cousins thought that the illness could be caused by unhappy thoughts. He did not want to take medicine to cure himself. Instead, he felt that happy thoughts or
15 laughter might cure his illness. He began to **experiment** on himself while still in the hospital by watching comedy shows on television. Mr. Cousins quickly found that ten minutes of real laughter during the day gave him two hours of **pain-free** sleep at night.

   Deciding that the doctors could not help him, Mr. Cousins left the hospital and
20 checked into a hotel room where he could continue his experiments with laughter. For eight days, Mr. Cousins rested in the hotel room watching comedy shows on television, reading **amusing** books, and sleeping whenever he felt tired. Within three weeks, he felt well enough to take a vacation to **Puerto Rico** where he began running on the beach for exercise. After a few months, Mr. Cousins was able to carry on his
25 work. He had laughed himself back to health.

328 words

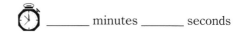 _____ minutes _____ seconds

Notes

saying「ことわざ」 **laughter**「笑い」 **editor**「編集者」 **world peace and anti-nuclear and anti-war issues**「世界平和や反核・反戦問題」 **ankylosing spondylitis**「強直性脊椎炎」（頸部・背部などが次第に動かなくなる病気） **pain-free**「痛みがない」 **Puerto Rico**「プエルトリコ」

READING COMPREHENSION

Circle the letter of the best answer.

1. What is the main topic of the passage?
   a. a funny story
   b. an interesting cure
   c. an amazing life
   d. why people laugh

2. What is NOT true about ankylosing spondylitis?
   a. It is uncommon.
   b. It makes walking difficult.
   c. It is easily cured.
   d. It is painful.

3. What did the doctors think about his disease?
   a. It could be cured if he slept more.
   b. It might never be cured.
   c. It could be cured by taking medicine.
   d. It would take a week to get over it.

4. What did Mr. Cousins think cured him?
   a. laughter
   b. running on the beach
   c. medicine
   d. taking a vacation

5. What did Mr. Cousins do after he got better?
   a. He went back to the hospital.
   b. He continued his job.
   c. He wrote amusing books.
   d. The passage doesn't say.

LISTENING COMPREHENSION   23

Listen to the CD and fill in the blanks.

Norman Cousins had a very strange (1)_____ which made his joints stiff, and it was (2)_____ for him to move around. Doctors could not (3)_____ his illness, and they said he may never (4)_____ it. But Mr. Cousins started to (5)_____ with laughter and he was finally able to get back to work.

VOCABULARY REINFORCEMENT

Circle the letter of the best answer.

1. Doug never exercises. I am worried about his _____.
   a. cure
   b. issue
   c. health
   d. experiment

2. Jo works as an _____ for a publishing company.
   a. article
   b. editor
   c. experiment
   d. explorer

3. Paul is really interested in _____ like saving nature.
   a. issues
   b. diseases
   c. experiments
   d. ceremonies

4. I am looking forward to _____ the hotel and having a shower.
   a. getting over
   b. checking into
   c. setting up
   d. watching out for

5. The train arrives at ten, so I'll probably _____ the office at 10:30.
   a. check out of
   b. set up
   c. get back to
   d. catch the eye of

IDIOMS

Find each idiom in the story and translate the sentences into Japanese.

1. (　　　) (　　　) = もどる
   Give me a call when you (　　　) (　　　) from your vacation.

2. (　　　) (　　　) = よくなる，回復する
   I feel terrible. I hope I (　　　) (　　　) this cold soon.

3. (　　　) (　　　) = (ホテルに) チェック・インする
   I had an early morning flight, so I (　　　) (　　　) the airport hotel. （過去形で）

Palm Reading

手相を見ましょう

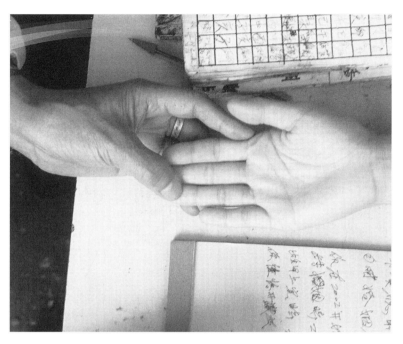

占いと言うと、何を思い浮かべますか。トランプ占い、星占い、そして手相占いがありますね。これまでに手相を見てもらったことがありますか。手相は人それぞれ異なります。占い師はその手相から何歳まで生きられるのか、いつ頃結婚するのかなどについて占います。あなたにはこれから英語の文を読む相が出ていますよ。

TARGET VOCABULARY

Look up each word in a dictionary and match it with the closest meaning.

1. _____ emotion ( ) a. the inside part of the hand with lines on it
2. _____ fate ( ) b. a feeling like happiness, sadness, excitement, etc.
3. _____ palm ( ) c. small; less important
4. _____ represent ( ) d. events that one cannot avoid in the future
5. _____ minor ( ) e. show; mean; stand for; replace

READING PASSAGE

1   Even for people who don't believe in **fortune telling**, it can be fun to learn about what fortune-tellers look at on a person's **palm**.

   To read a person's future, a fortune-teller looks at both of the person's hands. They say the hand that a person uses for writing will show the things the person has done in life and the choices he or she has made. Fortune-tellers say the person's other hand will show the abilities they were born with and their **fate**.

   In looking at each hand, fortune-tellers say that different lines on the hand **represent** things about a person's life. For example, they call the three major lines on people's hands **the head line**, **the heart line**, and **the life line**.

   The head line represents intelligence — people with a long head line are said to have an excellent memory, while those with a short one are very intelligent. The life line represents health, and the longer it is, the healthier someone is. The heart line represents **emotions** and relationships — as a rule, the longer it is, the more important relationships are to that person.

   Fortune-tellers also look at six **minor** lines, but quite a lot of people do not have one or more of the minor lines. The minor lines are said to represent things such as the person's fate, wealth, health, marriage life, and children. Fortune-tellers read these lines by looking at how deep and how long each line is.

   In addition, fortune-tellers believe they can read information from the fingers of the hand. Each finger has a certain skill or fortune related to it. The **thumb** is related to love, the **index finger** to leadership, the **middle finger** to fate, the **ring finger** to art and imagination, and **the smallest finger** to communication. A fortune-teller will look at the length of each finger, how the finger bends, the size of the joints, and the shape of the ends of the fingers.

327 words

Notes

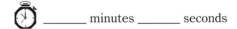 _____ minutes _____ seconds

fortune telling「占い」　**the head line**「頭脳線」　**the heart line**「感情線」　**the life line**「生命線」
thumb「親指」　**index finger**「人差し指」(forefinger とも言う.)　**middle finger**「中指」　**ring finger**「薬指」　**the smallest finger**「小指」(little finger とも言う.)

READING COMPREHENSION

Circle the letter of the best answer.

1. What is the main topic of the passage?
   a. how fortune-tellers read palms
   b. the history of palm reading
   c. a famous fortune-teller
   d. why palm reading is popular today

2. What should a fortune-teller look at to read a person's future?
   a. the back of the person's hand
   b. the fingers of the left hand
   c. the hand not used for writing
   d. the person's stronger hand

3. What is true about the minor lines on the palm?
   a. Some people might not have all of them.
   b. Few people are interested in these lines.
   c. The lines make the meaning of the fingers stronger.
   d. They are more difficult for fortune- tellers to read.

4. If a person has a long index finger with a good shape, which job would probably suit the person?
   a. actor
   b. manager
   c. journalist
   d. writer

5. Which is NOT important for reading palms?
   a. the depth of the lines
   b. the length of the fingers
   c. the size of the hand
   d. which hand is used

LISTENING COMPREHENSION   25

Listen to the CD and fill in the blanks.

Some people ask fortune-tellers to read their (1)_____ in order to find out their (2)_____. Fortune-tellers look at a person's fingers and the lines on both hands. There are three major lines on the hand, and several (3)_____ ones as well. These smaller lines (4)_____ such things as a person's wealth, marriage life, and (5)_____.

47

VOCABULARY REINFORCEMENT

Circle the letter of the word or phrase that best matches the words in *italics*.

1. She strongly *agrees with* giving money to other people.
   - a. believes in
   - b. is related to
   - c. hands out
   - d. represents

2. He tried not to show his *feelings*, but I knew he was sad.
   - a. thumbs
   - b. health
   - c. emotions
   - d. symptoms

3. The color white on the flag *stands for* the country's belief in peace and freedom.
   - a. founds
   - b. decreases
   - c. argues
   - d. represents

4. *Destiny*, not luck, brought them together and they fell in love.
   - a. Fate
   - b. Leadership
   - c. Interest
   - d. Atmosphere

5. It is important for a manager to have strong *directing and controlling* skills.
   - a. explosive
   - b. leadership
   - c. intelligent
   - d. complicated

IDIOMS

Find each idiom in the story and translate the sentences into Japanese.

1. (   ) (   ) = （本当であると）信じる
   I don't (   ) (   ) ghosts or witches.

2. (   ) (   ) (   ) (of) = たくさん，おおいに
   He has (   ) (   ) (   ) of money in the bank.

3. be (   ) (   ) = 〜と関係がある
   She said she is (   ) (   ) the Russian Royal family.

Amazing Memory

驚異の記憶力

contrast eventually poison journalist donation decade fact remove combine challenge perform record author novel break

暗証番号や電話番号など記憶しておかなければいけない数字があります。意味のない数字の羅列を覚えるときは語呂合わせをするとよいと言う人もいます。あなたが覚えている数字で最も長いものは何ですか。世の中には驚異的な記憶力を持つ人達がいます。彼らはどれくらいの数字を記憶することができたのでしょうか。

TARGET VOCABULARY

Look up each word in a dictionary and match it with the closest meaning.

1. _____ associate   (   ) a. remember something exactly (something with something)
2. _____ constant   (   ) b. the way things are arranged; sequence
3. _____ forever   (   ) c. connect something in the mind
4. _____ memorize   (   ) d. never-ending, for all time
5. _____ order   (   ) e. (adj.) not changing; (noun) a number that does not change

READING PASSAGE

1   Give this memory test a try. Take a **deck** of **playing cards** and mix them up. Now look at the top seven cards for a second each. Can you remember them in order? Contestants at the annual **World Memory Championships** can. In fact, the 2010 champion, **Wang Feng**, set a world record **memorizing** cards. Mr. Wang correctly remembered the random **order** of a deck of playing cards after looking at them for only 24 seconds! Unfortunately, Mr. Wang did not hold the record for long. The same year, **Simon Reinhardt** broke the record by memorizing the random order of the 52 cards in less than 22 seconds.

   Ben Pridmore, who won third place at the 2010 competition, also did something amazing. In only one hour, he memorized the order of 28 decks of cards. That is 1,456 cards!

   In 1987, a Japanese man, **Hideaki Tomoyori**, wanted to prove that his memory was the best in the world. So, he tried to remember by heart **pi** (π). This is a **constant** number in math which starts 3.14159 . . . It never repeats itself and never ends. He remembered pi to 40,000 decimal places. It took him more than twelve hours to say the numbers, but he did it without making a mistake!

   To remember pi, Mr. Tomoyori divided the number into groups of ten digits, and associated each number with a sound. He then made up stories to help him remember the words he made from the sounds. Mr. Tomoyori said that he first decided to memorize the value of pi up to 1,000 places, which took him three years. To get to 40,000 decimal places took about ten years.

   However, few records last **forever**. In 1995, **Hiroyuki Goto** memorized pi to 42,195 places. Ten years later, reports from China said **Lu Chao** managed to memorize pi to 67,890 places, but his record was soon broken by Akira Haraguchi who memorized pi to 83,431 places.

325 words

Notes

 _____ minutes _____ seconds

deck「一組の」　playing cards「トランプ」　World Memory Championship「記憶力世界一選手権」　Wang Feng「ワン・フェン」（中国人の大会優勝者．）　Simon Reinhardt「サイモン・ラインハルト」（ドイツ人の大会優勝者．）　Ben Pridmore「ベン・プリッドモア」（イギリス人の大会優勝者．）　Hideaki Tomoyori「友寄英哲」（日本人の円周率記憶の元世界記録保持者．）　pi「円周率」　Hiroyuki Goto「後藤裕之」（日本人の円周率記憶の元世界記録保持者．）　Lu Chao「呂超」（中国人の円周率記憶の元世界記録保持者．）　Akira Haraguchi「原口證」（日本人の円周率記憶の世界記録保持者．）

READING COMPREHENSION

Circle the letter of the best answer.

1. What is the best title for the passage?
   a. Great Memory Techniques
   b. Incredible Memorizers
   c. Strange Competitions
   d. Amazing Card Tricks

2. According to the passage, who holds the record for memorizing one deck of cards the fastest?
   a. Wang Feng
   b. Ben Pridmore
   c. Simon Reinhardt
   d. Hideaki Tomoyori

3. What is amazing about Mr. Pridmore?
   a. He won the competition three times.
   b. He beat Mr. Reinhardt's world record.
   c. He memorized a large number of cards.
   d. He remembered 1,456 different numbers.

4. What sentence is probably true about Hideaki Tomoyori?
   a. He has a good imagination.
   b. He only made one mistake.
   c. He found remembering pi quite easy.
   d. He has a better memory than Hiroyuki Goto.

5. Who remembered the greatest number of things or numbers?
   a. Hideaki Tomoyori
   b. Wang Feng
   c. Ben Pridmore
   d. Akira Haraguchi

LISTENING COMPREHENSION

Listen to the CD and fill in the blanks.

There are some people with amazing memory skills. One man memorized the order of thousands of (1)_____ cards after studying them for just one hour. Another man from Japan memorized pi (2)_____. This number is a mathematical (3)_____ that never repeats. To memorize this number, the man (4)_____ groups of numbers with sounds and words. Then he (5)_____ stories with these words to remember them. He memorized pi to 40,000 places this way.

VOCABULARY REINFORCEMENT

Circle the letter of the best answer.

1. Anne failed the test so she must _____ it. I hope she passes next time.
   a. forever
   b. associate
   c. memorize
   d. repeat

2. I know you aren't really into karaoke, but you should _____.
   a. give it a try
   b. carry on
   c. tie the knot
   d. make up

3. This concert seems to be going on _____. I hope it ends soon.
   a. random
   b. forever
   c. unfortunate
   d. for good

4. The children stood _____ from shortest to tallest.
   a. repeated
   b. related to
   c. in order
   d. associated

5. I have a lot of words to _____ for the test next week.
   a. by heart
   b. memorize
   c. train
   d. associate

IDIOMS

Find each idiom in the story and translate the sentences into Japanese.

1. (   ) (something) (   ) (   ) = 初めてやってみる
   You should (   ) snowboarding (   ) (   ). It's a lot of fun.

2. (   ) (   ) = 記憶して，そらで
   Colin remembered the poem (   ) (   ).

3. (   ) (   ) = 発明する，作り出す
   Blake loves (   ) (   ) stories to tell his children.

Incredible Dogs

ワンダフルわんちゃん

皆さんは家で犬を飼っていますか。犬種はたくさんあり、その形や大きさも様々です。写真の犬の種類がわかりますか。頭がよく、体が小さいことでも知られているヨークシャーテリアです。犬は家族と一緒に暮らし、飼い主を癒してくれます。ときには飼い主の命を救うこともあります。

TARGET VOCABULARY

Look up each word in a dictionary and match it with the closest meaning.

1. _____ wheelchair   ( ) a. someone that goes or lives with another person; friend
2. _____ bravery   ( ) b. not being afraid of danger
3. _____ companion   ( ) c. get better after being sick or injured
4. _____ documentary   ( ) d. a chair with wheels for people who cannot walk
5. _____ recover   ( ) e. a television show or movie based on true facts

READING PASSAGE

1   For thousands of years, people have lived with dogs. Ancient paintings on the walls of caves show people living with dogs. **More than one third** of the homes in the United States, Canada, and Australia have dogs. Almost one fourth of homes in England have dogs. In each country, these dogs **come in a wide variety of shapes and sizes**.

   The largest dog in the world was Zorba, a huge **mastiff** that passed away in 1990. When Zorba was seven years old in 1989, he was 94 centimeters (37 inches) tall. In other words, Zorba was more than half as tall as an adult man. At his largest, Zorba weighed more than a heavyweight boxer at 156 kilograms (343 pounds).

   In comparison, the smallest dog ever was a **Yorkshire terrier** named Sylvia from England. This dog was only the size of a matchbox, measuring just over six centimeters (2.5 inches) tall and just under nine centimeters (3.5 inches) from nose to tail. The dog weighed about half as much as this book, and even a young child could easily pick it up with one hand. It died in 1945 when it was only two years old.

   Some dogs are remarkable, not for their size, but for their brain. One incredible dog is Endal, the **companion** of a man named Allen Parton, who has used a **wheelchair** since a car accident in 1991.

   In 2001, Parton was hit by a car while crossing a road with Endal, and thrown out of his chair. Endal quickly moved Parton into the **recovery** position, covered him with a blanket, and pushed his mobile phone close enough for him to reach. Then, once he saw that Parton was all right, Endal ran back and forth to a nearby hotel, **barking** until people came out to help.

   Endal was rewarded for his **bravery** by being awarded a medal, and he has been the subject of a number of TV **documentaries**.

323 words

_____ minutes _____ seconds

Notes

more than one third「3分の1以上」 come in a wide variety of shapes and sizes「形から大きさまで多岐にわたる」 mastiff「マスチフ犬」(体重80kg前後の大型犬．性格はおおらかで飼い主に忠実．) Yorkshire terrier「ヨークシャーテリア」(体重3kg前後の小型室内犬．かわいい顔に長く美しい毛を持ち,「動く宝石」と呼ばれる．) bark「吠える」

READING COMPREHENSION

Circle the letter of the best answer.

1. What is the main topic of the passage?
   a. dogs that are special in some way
   b. three popular kinds of dogs
   c. dogs that have helped their owners
   d. the best dogs in a competition

2. According to the passage, why do people have dogs as pets?
   a. Dogs used to live in caves.
   b. Dogs come in all shapes and sizes.
   c. Dogs are great companions.
   d. The passage doesn't say.

3. Which sentence about Zorba is true?
   a. He was taller and heavier than an adult man.
   b. He was taller, but not heavier than an adult man.
   c. He was heavier, but not taller than an adult man.
   d. He was neither heavier nor taller than an adult man.

4. According to the passage, the world's smallest dog weighed as much as . . .
   a. a child's hand.
   b. half this book.
   c. a matchbox.
   d. Zorba.

5. Which is NOT true about Allen Parton?
   a. His dog has been on TV.
   b. He received a medal for bravery.
   c. He is unable to walk.
   d. He has been in at least two car accidents.

LISTENING COMPREHENSION 29

Listen to the CD and fill in the blanks.

Dogs are very popular pets, and they come in all shapes and sizes. Two of the most (1) _____ dogs were the largest dog in the world, Zorba, and the smallest dog, Sylvia. Zorba weighed more than a person. (2) _____ , Sylvia could easily be picked up by a young child. Another dog is famous not for its size, but for its (3)_____. Endal is the (4)_____ of a man who cannot walk and has to use a (5)_____. This brave dog saved the man's life after he was hit by a car.

VOCABULARY REINFORCEMENT

Circle the letter of the word or phrase that best matches the words in *italics*.

1. It took Brian almost six months to completely *get well* from his illness.
    a. pass away
    b. recover
    c. cure
    d. health

2. I saw a great *educational show* about Africa on TV last night.
    a. script
    b. scenery
    c. documentary
    d. companion

3. It was so cold last night I needed to get an extra *cover* for my bed.
    a. blanket
    b. feather
    c. order
    d. reward

4. Nathan gave *some money* to the person who found his wallet.
    a. a palm
    b. a bunch
    c. a bravery
    d. a reward

5. Takako is sad because her mother *died* last year.
    a. recovered
    b. passed away
    c. made up
    d. repeated

IDIOMS

Find each idiom in the story and translate the sentences into Japanese.

1. (   ) (   ) = 亡くなる
    I was sorry to hear that his father (   ) (   ). (過去形で)

2. (   ) (   ) = 比べると
    Sean looks really nervous. Ian, (   ) (   ), looks very relaxed.

3. (   ) (   ) (   ) = 行ったり来たり、あちこち
    The tennis players hit the ball (   ) (   ) (   ) for a long time.

Megacities

大都市

大都市と呼ばれる都市にはどのくらいの人が住んでいるのでしょうか。都市と大都市はどのようにして区別しているのでしょうか。日本で人口の多い都市と言えば、東京、横浜、大阪、名古屋、札幌が挙げられます。世界には大都市と呼ばれる都市がたくさんありますが、いくつ言えますか。

TARGET VOCABULARY

Look up each word in a dictionary and match it with the closest meaning.

1. _____ huge   ( ) a. area; part of (a country, state, province, etc.)
2. _____ consider   ( ) b. giant
3. _____ region   ( ) c. the number of people
4. _____ economic   ( ) d. related to earning and spending money
5. _____ population   ( ) e. think about

READING PASSAGE

1 Today, experts guess that over 50% of people worldwide live in cities. By the year 2050, they expect 70% are going to be living in cities. They also say that more of the world's cities will be **megacities** and mega-**regions**.

A megacity, as the name suggests, is a **huge** city. A basic **definition** might be any
5 city with over 10 million people. However, it is harder to count the actual number of people living in a city **than one might think**. For one thing, it is not always clear who to count. Many megacities do not have clear borders for where the city ends. Suburbs and regions around the city may or may not be included in the city's total **population**.

Even with the difficulty of saying where a city ends and who to count, it is clear that
10 certain cities around the world are megacities. **Sao Paulo**, the city with the most people in South America, is one. New York, the most famous city in North America, is another. Then there is Tokyo, a megacity with over 10 million people. This makes it the largest megacity in the world.

A mega-region, on the other hand, develops when megacities become so big we can
15 consider them to be connected. One report by the United Nations said the largest mega-region today is in China. The megacities included in this region are **Hong Kong**, **Shenzhen**, and **Guangzhou**. However, a mega-region does not have to be limited to one country. In West Africa, a mega-region connects four countries: **Nigeria**, **Benin**, **Togo**, and **Ghana**.

20 An important fact about mega-regions is how much **economic** power they have. Research by the United Nations found that 66% of economic activity worldwide happened within the world's 40 largest mega-regions. The research also showed that 85% of new ideas in technology and science came from these 40 mega-regions. Less than 20% of the world's population, however, lives in these mega-regions.

321 words

Notes ⏱ _____ minutes _____ seconds

megacity「大都市」 definition「定義」 than one might think「人が考えているよりも」 Sao Paulo「サンパウロ」（ブラジルの都市.） Hong Kong「香港」 Shenzhen「深圳」（中国の都市.） Guangzhou「広州」（中国の都市.） Nigeria「ナイジェリア」 Benin「ベナン」 Togo「トーゴ」 Ghana「ガーナ」

READING COMPREHENSION

Circle the letter of the best answer.

1. What is the best title for the passage?
   a. Good Things about Living in Cities
   b. Problems with Too Many People
   c. Growing Cities and Regions
   d. The City with the Highest Population

2. Why is it hard to count the population living in megacities?
   a. Defining the border of the city is hard.
   b. People are born every day.
   c. More people move to the cities.
   d. The suburbs grow too quickly.

3. Which of the following cities is NOT listed as a megacity in the passage?
   a. London
   b. Sao Paulo
   c. New York
   d. Tokyo

4. How are mega-regions defined in the passage?
   a. connected megacities
   b. large areas with many suburbs
   c. places with 10 million people
   d. countries with three or more megacities

5. What is NOT true about mega-regions?
   a. Most new ideas in science and technology come from them.
   b. One-third of the world's population lives in them.
   c. Two-thirds of the world's economic activity happens in them
   d. There is a mega-region in Africa.

LISTENING COMPREHENSION 31

Listen to the CD and fill in the blanks.

Around the world, cities are growing and some experts now consider some places to be megacities. As (1)_____ , a megacity is a city that is very large and has a (2)_____ of more than 10 million people. Actually, it (3)_____ to count the number of people living in a huge city than one thinks. That is because it is not always easy to define where the border of the city should be. Another way that (4)_____ look at cities and countries today is by defining mega-regions. These are (5)_____ with several megacities connected physically and economically.

59

VOCABULARY REINFORCEMENT

Circle the letter of the best answer.

1. The country has a serious _____ problem. People there can't even buy food.
   a. expert
   b. total
   c. economic
   d. huge

2. I love this song. I can sing the whole thing _____ for you.
   a. by heart
   b. in comparison
   c. quite a lot of
   d. expert

3. Many lakes can be found in the southern _____ of the country.
   a. bravery
   b. expert
   c. population
   d. region

4. We are _____ only 30 minutes for our lunch break.
   a. hard to find
   b. related to
   c. limited to
   d. considered

5. Anyone can easily cross the _____ between the two countries.
   a. border
   b. companion
   c. definition
   d. suburb

IDIOMS

Find each idiom in the story and translate the sentences into Japanese.

1. ( ) ( ) ( ) ( ) = その名が示すように
   ( ) ( ) ( ) ( ), global warming refers to the trend of rising average global temperatures.

2. (be) ( ) ( ) (one) ( ) = （人が）思っているよりも難しい
   Passing my driving test was ( ) ( ) I ( ).

3. ( ) ( ) ( ) = 〜に限られる，だけである
   My family's vacation plans ( ) ( ) ( ) visiting relatives or going to the beach near our house. （過去形で）

Space Explorers

宇宙飛行士

十年一昔という言葉がありますが、宇宙飛行に関してはまさにその言葉が当てはまります。人類が月に着陸してから何十年かの間に巨大な宇宙ステーションで暮らせるようにまでなりました。現在では、火星に住むプロジェクトも民間会社によって計画されているようです。もし機会があったら、あなたは宇宙に行ってみたいですか。

TARGET VOCABULARY

Look up each word in a dictionary and match it with the closest meaning.

1. _____ aboard   ( ) a. a person who goes into space
2. _____ astronaut   ( ) b. send up into the air, or into space
3. _____ launch   ( ) c. an object sent into space as part of a
                                      communication system
4. _____ mission   ( ) d. on a ship, train, plane, or other vehicle
5. _____ satellite   ( ) e. an important job that a group of people are sent
                                      to do somewhere

READING PASSAGE

1   After men landed on the moon in 1969, **astronauts** around the world had a problem — there were no other places they could go! Even today, the other planets are still too far away for astronauts to fly to. So, while rockets and robots can go to other planets, flights with astronauts have to stay closer to home, at least for the time being.

5   Therefore, since visiting the moon, manned space programs have turned their attention to solving problems related to living and working in space. For the past **decade**, **NASA**'s manned space exploration program focused on the **space shuttle** program. During that time, NASA operated three space shuttles: Discovery, Atlantis, and Endeavor. Unfortunately, two of NASA's shuttles, Challenger and Columbia, were lost through
10 accidents. Seven astronauts died in each accident. While the shuttle program was going on, the shuttles flew over 120 **missions**. These missions included putting **satellites** into orbit, photographing the earth, studying space, conducting experiments related to working in space, and connecting with various manned space stations in orbit. Today, however, Discovery, Atlantis, and Endeavor are no longer being flown. NASA retired its space shuttle
15 program in 2011.

    As well as rockets and space shuttles, several space stations have been put into orbit. In 1986, the Soviet Union **launched the Mir space station**. Mir stayed in orbit until March 23, 2001. Over that time, 104 astronauts visited the station to stay for various lengths of time.

20 The person who has spent the longest in space so far is Russian astronaut **Sergei Krikalev**. Working **aboard** Mir and flying in other missions, Mr. Krikalev lived and worked in space for a total of 803 days, 9 hours, and 39 minutes. That is more than two years in space.

    Another space station, **the International Space Station** (ISS), is still in orbit today.
25 The first part of this space station was launched in 1998. NASA added the final section to the ISS in 2010, officially completing the space station. In the long run, it is predicted that research done aboard the ISS will help scientists learn about living and working in space.

                                                                                       356 words

Notes

decade「10年間」 NASA「アメリカ航空宇宙局」(惑星探査計画やスペースシャトル計画などの宇宙計画の推進機関.) space shuttle「スペースシャトル」(宇宙と地球間の往復ができるアメリカの有人ロケット.) the Mir space station「ミール宇宙ステーション」(全長約18メートルのロシアの宇宙ステーション.) Sergei Krikalev「セルゲイ・クリカレフ」(宇宙滞在最長記録を保持するロシア人宇宙飛行士.) the International Space Station「国際宇宙ステーション」(国際協力によって完成した全長73メートルの宇宙ステーション.)

READING COMPREHENSION

Circle the letter of the best answer.

1. What is the best title for the passage?
    a. Sergei Krikalev — An Amazing Astronaut
    b. The Past and Future of Space Travel
    c. Space Cities of the Future
    d. Living and Working on the International Space Station

2. According to the passage, why are astronauts unable to travel to other planets now?
    a. There are not enough space shuttles.
    b. There have been too many rocket accidents.
    c. There are too many problems here on Earth
    d. The journey would take too long for a person.

3. How many space shuttle astronauts have been killed in accidents?
    a. 2
    b. 7
    c. 14
    d. 120

4. What is NOT true about Sergei Krikalev?
    a. He is an astronaut from Russia.
    b. He spent more than two years aboard Mir.
    c. He has been on many space missions.
    d. He has spent more time in space than anyone else.

5. What is true about the International Space Station?
    a. It was built by the United States alone.
    b. It was launched into space in 2010.
    c. NASA completed it in 1998.
    d. Scientists will do research aboard it.

LISTENING COMPREHENSION

Listen to the CD and fill in the blanks.

It is not yet possible for people to travel to other (1) _____ by rocket because they are so far away. Therefore, space programs today focus on developing safe ways for (2) _____ to live and work in space. One way space programs can (3) _____ experiments on living and working in space is by putting space stations in orbit. The Russian space station Mir was (4) _____ into orbit in 1986, and it stayed up for more than ten years. One astronaut who spent time (5) _____ Mir, Sergei Krikalev, has spent more time in space than any other person!

VOCABULARY REINFORCEMENT

Circle the letter of the word or phrase that best matches the words in *italics*.

1. I've been studying all morning, but *up to now* I've only memorized fifteen words.
   a. by heart
   b. so far
   c. in the long run
   d. for the time being

2. Maria would love to retire, but she needs the money, so *for now* she has to keep working.
   a. even though
   b. so far
   c. for one thing
   d. for the time being

3. He is a terrible fortune-teller. Nothing he *says* comes true.
   a. conducts
   b. recovers
   c. captures
   d. predicts

4. The President sent a team of experts on an important *assignment* to try to end the war.
   a. satellite
   b. documentary
   c. mission
   d. security

5. This car is very expensive, but it will drive well for many years, and *over time* you will save money.
   a. in the long run
   b. so far
   c. even though
   d. for the time being

IDIOMS

Find each idiom in the story and translate the sentences into Japanese.

1. (　　) (　　) (　　) (　　) = 今は，今のところ
   The fighting between the two countries has stopped (　　) (　　) (　　) (　　).

2. (　　) (　　) = 今まで，今のところ
   I love traveling. (　　) (　　), I've been to 53 countries.

3. (　　) (　　) (　　) (　　) = 長い目で見れば，結局は
   Smoking is very bad for your health (　　) (　　) (　　) (　　).

64

Happy New Year!
ハッピーニューイヤー

新年の祝い方は国によって異なります。正月の時期が異なる国もあるようです。日本では門松や注連飾りを飾り、元日におせち料理を食べ、初詣をしたりしますね。最近では、年賀状のかわりにメールを送る人もいます。外国では新年をどのように祝っているのでしょうか。

TARGET VOCABULARY

Look up each word in a dictionary and match it with the closest meaning.

1. _____ gown   ( ) a. like more
2. _____ habit   ( ) b. say you will do something
3. _____ prefer   ( ) c. a long formal dress
4. _____ promise   ( ) d. something someone does often
5. _____ widespread   ( ) e. common; found or happening in many places

READING PASSAGE 🎧 34

1   Almost all cultures celebrate the end of one year and the beginning of another in some way. Different cultures celebrate the beginning of a new year in different ways, and at different times on the calendar.

     In Western countries, people usually celebrate New Year at midnight on December
5 31st. People may go to parties, sometimes **dressed in formal clothes** such as **tuxedos** and evening **gowns**, and they may drink champagne at midnight. During the first minutes of the new year, people cheer and wish each other happiness for the year ahead. But some cultures **prefer** to celebrate the new year by waking up early to watch the sun rise. They welcome the new year with the first light of the sunrise.

10   It is also a common Western custom to make a New Year's promise, called a **resolution**. New Year's resolutions usually include promises to try something new or change a bad **habit** in the new year.

     Many cultures also do special things to **get rid of** bad luck at the beginning of a new year. For example, in **Ecuador**, families make a big doll from old clothes. The doll is
15 filled with old newspapers and **firecrackers**. At midnight, these dolls are burned to show the bad things from the past year are gone and the new year can start afresh. Other common traditions to keep away bad luck in a new year include throwing things into rivers or the ocean, or saying special things on the first day of the new year.

     Other New Year traditions are followed to bring good luck in the new year. One
20 **widespread** Spanish tradition for good luck is to eat grapes on New Year's Day. The more grapes a person eats, the more good luck the person will have in the year. In France, people eat pancakes for good luck at New Year. In the United States, some people eat **black-eyed peas** for good luck — but to get good luck for a whole year you have to eat 365 of them!

338 words

Notes

⏱ _____ minutes _____ seconds

dress in formal clothes「正装する」 tuxedo「タキシード」 resolution「決意」 get rid of「取り除く」 Ecuador「エクアドル」 firecracker「爆竹」 black-eyed peas「ササゲ（大角豆）」

READING COMPREHENSION

Circle the letter of the best answer.

1. What is the main idea of the passage
   a. the meaning of "Happy New Year!"
   b. what date New Year is celebrated
   c. various New Year traditions
   d. why people make resolutions in different cultures

2. Which culture celebrates New Year in the morning?
   a. the United States
   b. Spain
   c. Ecuador
   d. The passage doesn't say.

3. What is a resolution?
   a. something you burn
   b. something you eat
   c. something you say you will do
   d. something you wear

4. What is the topic of the fourth paragraph?
   a. bringing good luck
   b. keeping away bad luck
   c. planning for the next year
   d. remembering the past

5. Which is probably true about eating black-eyed peas on New Year?
   a. Black-eyed peas taste bad.
   b. One pea brings one day of luck.
   c. The peas are very difficult to cook.
   d. It is bad luck to eat a lot of black-eyed peas.

LISTENING COMPREHENSION

Listen to the CD and fill in the blanks.

New Year is celebrated around the world through many different customs. In many Western countries, quite a lot of people go to parties in the (1) _____ wearing formal clothes, like tuxedos and (2) _____ . In other cultures, people (3)_____ to get up early and watch the sun rise. Many cultures also have New Year traditions to (4)_____ bad luck and (5)_____ in the new year.

VOCABULARY REINFORCEMENT

Circle the letter of the best answer.

1. Young children should _____ the swimming pool when no adults are there.
   a. get rid of
   b. keep away from
   c. break into
   d. keep an eye on

2. It's already a new month! I need to turn over my _____.
   a. calendar
   b. habit
   c. gown
   d. resolution

3. Please _____ you will not tell anyone my secret.
   a. prefer
   b. disguise
   c. argue
   d. promise

4. Most people think that smoking is a terrible _____.
   a. habit
   b. fate
   c. resolution
   d. explosive

5. That disease is _____ now. It kills millions of people around the world every year.
   a. rare
   b. formal
   c. brave
   d. widespread

IDIOMS

Find each idiom in the story and translate the sentences into Japanese.

1. (   ) (   ) (   ) = 捨てる，取り除く
   She (   ) (   ) (   ) her old car and bought a motorbike. （過去形で）

2. (   ) (   ) = やりなおす，もう一度はじめる
   I didn't like what I had written, so I (   ) (   ). （過去形で）

3. (   ) (   ) = 離れている，近づけない
   (   ) (   ) from the stove! It's hot!

Rain
レイン

写真の男性が誰だかわかりますか。韓国人歌手のレインです。彼は韓国のほか、アジアやアメリカで活躍しています。また、歌だけではなく、TVドラマや映画にも出演しています。彼が歌手になる夢をどう叶え、活躍しているのか読んでみましょう。

TARGET VOCABULARY

Look up each word in a dictionary and match it with the closest meaning.

1. _____ album   ( ) a. many songs sold together as one product
2. _____ brand   ( ) b. kind or make related to a certain company
3. _____ drama   ( ) c. put out; offer for sale to the public
4. _____ producer   ( ) d. a show that is serious or sad
5. _____ release   ( ) e. the person who is mainly responsible for making an album, a movie, a TV show, etc.

READING PASSAGE

1   When **Rain** was growing up, he had big dreams. He wanted to become a famous singer and dancer. He worked hard and made his first solo **album** when he was 20 years old. Rain did not stop there. Today, he is known as a dancer, singer, actor, and businessman!

5   In high school, Jeong Ji-Hun (Rain) was part of a singing group called Fan Club. The group made two albums before they broke up. Rain tried to find **work as a dancer** in the music industry. Then in 1999, he caught the eye of a famous singer and **producer**, **Park Jin-Young**. Mr. Park worked with Rain for several years, helping the young man develop his dancing and singing skills.

10   Things really started happening for Rain after his first album, *Bad Guy*, was **released** in Korea in 2002. That same year, he acted in two television comedies. In 2003, his album *How to Avoid the Sun* was released and he also acted in another TV series called *Sang Doo! Let Us Go To School!* The next year, Rain became famous across Asia starring in the hit TV **drama** *Full House* and releasing his third album,
15   *It's Raining*. Soon after that, Rain gave many international concerts, including one in New York.

Rain also managed to find the time to **star in** his first Korean movie in 2006: *I'm a Cyborg, But It's Okay*. Two years later, he had a role in *Speed Racer*, his first Hollywood movie. And in 2009, he **played the main role** in the Hollywood action
20   movie *Ninja Assassin*.

With all of that work, it is hard to imagine that Rain had time to do anything else, but he also found the time to start his own businesses. He started his own music company, which released his fifth album, *Rainism*, in 2008. He started another company the same year to make the clothes **brand** "Six to Five."

317 words

Notes

Rain「レイン」（韓国人歌手・俳優・実業家．本名チョン・ジフン．「ピ」（韓国語で雨の意味）とも呼ばれる．） work as a dancer「ダンサーとしての仕事」 Park Jin-Young「パク・ジニョン」（韓国の音楽プロデューサー．） star in「～に主演する」 play the main role「主役を演じる」

READING COMPREHENSION

Circle the letter of the best answer.

1. What is the main topic of the passage?
   a. a man who does many things
   b. a singer's different styles
   c. an actor who became a singer
   d. how rain helped a singer

2. What is the writer's opinion?
   a. Acting in movies is harder than acting on TV.
   b. Rain's fifth album was his best one.
   c. Rain is a hard-working artist.
   d. The movies Rain starred in made him famous.

3. What was Fan Club?
   a. a dancing program on TV
   b. people who liked Jeong Ji-Hun's music
   c. a group of singers
   d. the producer of Rain's first album

4. According to the passage, which of the following has Rain NOT done?
   a. performed concerts in London
   b. starred in a hit TV series
   c. recorded a solo album
   d. worked as a dancer

5. In which industry does Rain own a company?
   a. fashion
   b. food
   c. movie
   d. television

LISTENING COMPREHENSION

Listen to the CD and fill in the blanks.

Rain began his career as a singer in high school, but the singing group (1)_____ after making two albums. Rain did not give up his dream. He (2)_____ meet a producer who helped him develop his talent. After he released his first solo (3)_____, he went on to star in a television drama series. Later, he played the main (4)_____ in a Hollywood movie. But he kept singing and making albums, too. Today, Rain is also a businessman. He owns the company called "Six to Five" that makes clothes. It is (5)_____ a more hard-working entertainer!

71

VOCABULARY REINFORCEMENT

Circle the letter of the word or phrase that best matches the words in *italics*.

1. I don't want to buy the *CD* because I only like one song on it.
   - a. album
   - b. drama
   - c. habit
   - d. gown

2. I found some DVDs of that old TV *program* you like.
   - a. role
   - b. mission
   - c. population
   - d. series

3. For most people, the problems of a child star are *difficult to understand*.
   - a. kept away
   - b. gotten rid of
   - c. hard to imagine
   - d. managing to do it

4. The small store did not carry my favorite *kind* of cola.
   - a. habit
   - b. brand
   - c. star
   - d. role

5. Our team has a better chance of succeeding if we do not *stop working with each other* but stay together.
   - a. hard to imagine
   - b. break up
   - c. keep away
   - d. manage to do

IDIOMS

Find each idiom in the story and translate the sentences into Japanese.

1. (   ) (   ) = 解散する

   The four women were in a band together, but the band (   ) (   ) last year.（過去形で）

2. (   ) (   ) = なんとかやり遂げる

   He (   ) (   ) finish his essay by staying up all night writing it.（過去形で）

3. (be) (   ) (   ) (   ) = 想像しにくい

   Big buildings were (   ) (   ) (   ) when New York was founded in the 1600s.

72

Urban Legends

都市伝説はホント？　ウソ？

都市伝説と聞くとどんな伝説を思い出しますか。例えば、アメリカのエリア51と呼ばれる空軍基地内に宇宙人が保管されているだとか、口裂け女がいて云々など聞いたことがあるかもしれません。都市伝説はどんなものがあるのでしょうか。また、どうして都市伝説は生まれるのでしょうか。

TARGET VOCABULARY

Look up each word in a dictionary and match it with the closest meaning.

1. _____ bizarre　　　(　) a. easy and clear to see and understand
2. _____ legend　　　 (　) b. very strange or unusual
3. _____ obvious　　　(　) c. become smaller
4. _____ shrink　　　 (　) d. related to a city
5. _____ urban　　　　(　) e. a story or myth, usually from long ago

READING PASSAGE

1   Have you heard about the woman who put her wet dog in the microwave to dry it, and ended up cooking her dog **by mistake**? Or did you hear about the man who died at his desk at work, and nobody in the office noticed he was dead for five days? These stories have two things in common. They are not true and they are **urban legends**.

5   Urban legends are usually stories about things that happened recently and took place in cities or in places well known to people. Another characteristic of urban legends is that there are many different versions of the same story, with local information changed to make the story seem more real. Today, the Internet has become a common way for urban legends to spread very quickly.

10   Some stories that sound like urban legends actually start from bizarre real events. For example, there is a story about **muggers** using snakes to rob people. There have been real reports about muggers doing this. The muggers **threaten** a victim by holding a snake in the person's face. Then the robber takes the victim's money. According to legend, these robbers are very common, so you should keep an eye out
15 for strangers carrying snakes.

Other urban legends **have been around** for a long time, and many people just believe them as facts. A good example of this kind of urban legend is related to **the Great Wall of China**. The myth is that the Great Wall can be seen from the moon. However, astronauts who have been to the moon say that even the size of countries
20 **shrinks** too much at that distance. It is **obvious** to most people, when they think about it, that from the moon it is impossible to see cities or things built by man, but some people believe the Great Wall can be seen from orbit above the Earth. However, this is also a myth. Shuttle astronaut Jay Apt looked for it but could not find it. He reported seeing airports, but he couldn't see the Great Wall. He guessed that was
25 because it was almost the same color as the land around it.

360 words

Notes   _____ minutes _____ seconds

by mistake「間違って」 **urban legend**「都市伝説」(現代の話題で事実が確認できない噂.) **mugger**「強盗」 **threaten**「脅す」 **have been around**「(過去のある時点から今に至るまで) 存在している」 **the Great Wall of China**「中国の万里の長城」(中国の城壁の遺跡. 世界遺産.)

READING COMPREHENSION

Circle the letter of the best answer.

1. What is the best title for the passage?
   a. Amazing True Stories
   b. Legends through History
   c. Bizarre Crimes
   d. Bizarre Stories

2. What is NOT true about urban legends?
   a. They usually take place in the country, or in small towns.
   b. There is usually more than one version of the legend.
   c. They are sometimes based on a real event.
   d. The Internet has made urban legends more widespread.

3. According to the passage, what do muggers do with snakes?
   a. send them into locked rooms
   b. throw them into people's cars
   c. show them to people
   d. give them to children

4. What is an urban myth about the Great Wall of China described in the passage?
   a. It was made by aliens.
   b. It is the size of a country.
   c. It was used to study the moon.
   d. It can be seen from space.

5. Which story in the passage really happened?
   a. the dog in the microwave
   b. the dead man in the office
   c. the astronaut who saw the Great Wall from space
   d. the muggers who threaten victims with snakes

LISTENING COMPREHENSION

CD 39

Listen to the CD and fill in the blanks.

If you have (1)_____ muggers using snakes to rob people, then you have heard an urban (2)_____ . Most urban legends have several characteristics (3)_____. There are usually several different (4)_____ of the same story. They often take place in urban areas, and because they sound (5)_____, but not obviously untrue, many people believe them completely.

75

VOCABULARY REINFORCEMENT

Circle the letter of the best answer.

1. There is a traditional Japanese _____ about Momotaro, the Peach Boy.
    a. article
    b. essay
    c. legend
    d. urban

2. That question on the test was too easy. The answer was _____ to everyone.
    a. obvious
    b. complicated
    c. bizarre
    d. random

3. Harvey _____ to quit his job if he did not get more money.
    a. evolved
    b. threatened
    c. launched
    d. limited

4. When you're at the shopping mall today, _____ any bargains.
    a. keep your eye on
    b. hear about
    c. break into
    d. keep an eye out for

5. In many countries, people are leaving farms and moving to _____ areas.
    a. urban
    b. obvious
    c. widespread
    d. common

IDIOMS

Find each idiom in the story and translate the sentences into Japanese.

1. (　　　) (　　　) = （人や物事）についてくわしく聞く
   How did you (　　　) (　　　) this restaurant?

2. (　　　) (something) (　　　) (　　　) = 〜を共有している
   The only thing the students in this class (　　　) (　　　) (　　　) is their need to learn English.

3. (　　　) (　　　) (　　　) (　　　) (　　　) = 注意深く見守る, 注意して見る
   Whenever I'm in a bookstore, I (　　　) (　　　) (　　　) (　　　) (　　　) interesting new books.

Extreme Sports

極限のスポーツ

皆さんはどのスポーツを見るのが好きですか。いろんな競技を見ることができるスポーツの祭典と言えば、オリンピックが代表的ですが、最近若い人に人気の高い新スポーツの祭典があるようです。その祭典ではどのような競技が競われるのか読んでみましょう。

TARGET VOCABULARY

Look up each word in a dictionary and match it with the closest meaning.

1. _____ junior　　　　( ) a. younger
2. _____ convince　　 ( ) b. far from normal; far from the center
3. _____ demonstrate ( ) c. show how to do something
4. _____ encourage　 ( ) d. make others believe that something is true or a good idea
5. _____ extreme　　 ( ) e. give strength or hope to someone; help someone to do something

READING PASSAGE

1   In the summer of 1993, Ron Semaio, director of programming for the U.S. sports cable channel **ESPN**, came up with an idea for a new sports program. While he was watching television one afternoon, Semaio started to think about how much young people liked to do extreme sports, such as skateboarding, snowboarding, and **BMX bike** racing. He thought of an event where people could watch **athletes** compete in these sports in a kind of **extreme** Olympics.

   It took some time to **convince** the management at ESPN that the idea showed promise, and then it took even longer to organize the competition. Finally, in the summer of 1995, the first Extreme Games took place in **Rhode Island** in the United States. More than 350 athletes from around the world came to compete in events such as bungee jumping, barefoot waterskiing, windsurfing, BMX biking, skateboarding, and climbing. The competitions were shown on ESPN and were a big hit, especially with males between 12 and 30 years old.

   The success of the first show resulted in the competition becoming an annual event. The second year, ESPN renamed the competition the X Games. The **organizers** also announced that they would hold a winter X Games that year. In the winter games, athletes competed in BMX racing on snow, snowboarding, ice climbing, and various ski competitions.

   That same year, a few athletes were also asked to travel to Brazil and China to **demonstrate** their skill and to stir up interest in the X Games in those countries. The touring X Games show became known as the X Trials. New athletes could compete in the X Trials, and if they did well, they were then allowed to compete in the X Games. In addition to the X Games held in the United States each year, today there are also the Asian X Games, a Latin X Games, and a **Junior** X Games to **encourage** young athletes to compete in extreme sports.

325 words

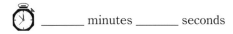 _____ minutes _____ seconds

Notes

ESPN [Entertainment and Sports Programming Network] (アメリカのスポーツ専門ケーブルテレビ局. 野球・サッカー・バスケット・アメフトなどを24時間放送.)　**athlete**「選手」　**Rhode Island**「ロードアイランド」(アメリカ東北部の州.)　**organizer**「主催者」　**BMX bike**「モトクロス用自転車」(荒地での走行やレースでの使用を目的とした自転車.)

READING COMPREHENSION

Circle the letter of the best answer.

1. What is the main topic of the passage?
    a. the life of Ron Semaio
    b. famous athletes in extreme sports
    c. the dangers of extreme sports
    d. the history of the X Games

2. Where did the first Extreme Games take place?
    a. Brazil
    b. the USA
    c. China
    d. The article doesn't say.

3. Which group was probably the largest group watching the first X Games?
    a. young men
    b. teenage girls
    c. men over 30
    d. women in their 20s

4. Which was held first?
    a. Junior X Games
    b. Summer X Games
    c. Winter X Games
    d. Extreme Games

5. In which paragraph does the writer describe how the X Games first became popular?
    a. paragraph 1
    b. paragraph 2
    c. paragraph 3
    d. paragraph 4

LISTENING COMPREHENSION   41

Listen to the CD and fill in the blanks.

The X Games is a competition for athletes in (1)_____ sports. In addition to the X Games, and the (2)_____ X Games (for younger athletes), there is also the X Trials, where competitors in the X Games travel to other countries to (3)_____ interest in the competition. In addition, if new athletes (4)_____ in the X Trials, this might (5)_____ them going on to compete in the X Games.

79

VOCABULARY REINFORCEMENT

Circle the letter of the word or phrase that best matches the words in *italics*.

1. He *showed* his skill at walking on his hands.
    a. demonstrated
    b. encouraged
    c. organized
    d. convinced

2. Alice didn't want to come to the party, but I managed to *change her thinking*.
    a. threaten her
    b. shrink her
    c. organize her
    d. convince her

3. Fiona is so good at sports because her parents really *gave her hope* when she was young.
    a. demonstrated her
    b. experimented her
    c. launched her
    d. encouraged her

4. I don't like to play sports, and I *really* don't like to play basketball.
    a. probably
    b. especially
    c. unfortunately
    d. eventually

5. His friends are *putting together* a surprise party for him.
    a. organizing
    b. inviting
    c. convincing
    d. limiting

IDIOMS

Find each idiom in the story and translate the sentences into Japanese.

1. (　　　) (　　　) = 有望である，見込みがある
    I didn't (　　　) any (　　　) at soccer, so I gave it up.

2. (　　　) (　　　) = 引き起こす，結果として〜になる
    Your bad diet will surely (　　　) (　　　) health problems in the future.

3. (　　　) (　　　) = 興奮させる，かき立てる
    The speaker (　　　) (　　　) the emotions of the crowd.（過去形で）

WPM 記録シート

時間を計りながら全体の内容を短時間で読み取る速読をしてみましょう。本文の最後に単語数が掲載されています。読み終えたら、単語数を読むのにかかった時間で割ります。例えば、300語の文を6分で読み終えた場合、300語÷6分＝分速50語（WPM）です。毎回、WPMを記録しておけば、速読力の伸びがわかります。

Unit	単語数	読了時間	WPM	50	100	150	200
記入例	300	6:00	50.0	●			
Unit 1	341	:					
Unit 2	319	:					
Unit 3	310	:					
Unit 4	374	:					
Unit 5	315	:					
Unit 6	333	:					
Unit 7	336	:					
Unit 8	290	:					
Unit 9	323	:					
Unit 10	299	:					
Unit 11	328	:					
Unit 12	327	:					
Unit 13	325	:					
Unit 14	323	:					
Unit 15	321	:					
Unit 16	356	:					
Unit 17	338	:					
Unit 18	317	:					
Unit 19	360	:					
Unit 20	325	:					

TEXT PRODUCTION STAFF

edited by Eiichi Kanno	編集 菅野 英一
English-language editing by Bill Benfield	英文校閲 ビル・ベンフィールド
cover design by Fumio Takahashi (AZ)	表紙デザイン 高橋文雄（AZ）

CD PRODUCTION STAFF

recorded by Katie Adler (AmE) Chris Wells (AmE)	吹き込み者 ケイティー・アドラー（アメリカ英語） クリス・ウェルズ（アメリカ英語）

Intermediate Faster Reading —New Edition—
速読の実践演習―最新版―

2016年1月20日　初版　発行
2025年3月15日　第5刷　発行

著　者　Casey Malarcher
　　　　原田 慎一

発行者　佐野 英一郎

発行所　株式会社 成美堂
　　　　〒101-0052　東京都千代田区神田小川町3-22
　　　　TEL 03-3291-2261　FAX 03-3293-5490
　　　　https://www.seibido.co.jp

印刷・製本　三美印刷（株）

ISBN 978-4-7919-4781-2　　　　　　　　　　　Printed in Japan

・落丁・乱丁本はお取り替えします。
・本書の無断複写は、著作権上の例外を除き著作権侵害となります。